Minecraft Modding with Forge

WITHDRAWN

Arun Gupta and Aditya Gupta

Beijing · Cambridge · Farnham · Köln · Sebastopol · Tokyo

Minecraft Modding with Forge

by Arun Gupta and Aditya Gupta

Printed in the United States of America.

Published by O'Reilly Media, Inc., 1005 Gravenstein Highway North, Sebastopol, CA 95472.

O'Reilly books may be purchased for educational, business, or sales promotional use. Online editions are also available for most titles (*http://safaribooksonline.com*). For more information, contact our corporate/institutional sales department: 800-998-9938 or *corporate@oreilly.com*.

Editors: Brian Foster and Brian MacDonald	**Indexer:** Lucie Haskins
Production Editor: Kristen Brown	**Interior Designer:** David Futato
Copyeditor: Jasmine Kwityn	**Cover Designer:** Karen Montgomery
Proofreader: Sharon Wilkey	**Illustrator:** Rebecca Demarest

April 2015:   First Edition

Revision History for the First Edition

2015-03-31:   First Release

See *http://oreilly.com/catalog/errata.csp?isbn=9781491918890* for release details.

The O'Reilly logo is a registered trademark of O'Reilly Media, Inc. *Minecraft Modding with Forge*, the cover image of a Texas horned lizard, and related trade dress are trademarks of O'Reilly Media, Inc.

978-1-491-91889-0

[LSI]

Table of Contents

Foreword

Learning how to code is an important life skill for today's youth. It not only provides them with a greater understanding of the computers and software that surround us all in our daily lives, but also has the potential to lead them toward an amazing and fulfilling career in technology. The genius of the Minecraft modding community is that it is helping to teach an enormous number of young programmers that coding can be fun. The ability to enhance and modify a game enjoyed by millions makes coding something that is approachable and enjoyable for kids of all ages.

The Eclipse Java IDE is one of the world's most successful open source software projects. Millions of developers use Eclipse every day as their tooling platform. The Eclipse community has hundreds of dedicated committers and thousands of contributors. Speaking on their behalf, it is incredibly gratifying for all of us to see our open source Eclipse IDE being used to help so many young people get started with coding.

As a father-and-son team, Arun Gupta and Aditya Gupta have created an incredible resource to help get this next generation of coders off to a great start. Arun is a well-known and respected Java technology evangelist who has held positions at Sun, Oracle, and Red Hat. Both he and Aditya have been active for several years in the Minecraft and Devoxx4Kids communities, helping to demonstrate that Java, Eclipse, and Minecraft modding are approachable and fun. I am sure that their book will provide you with a great start for your coding adventures.

—Mike Milinkovich, Executive Director of the Eclipse Foundation

Preface

One day a couple of years ago, I was stunned when my son told me, "Dad, my JAR snapshot messed up the configuration." As a curious dad and an experienced Java programmer, my question to him was, "How do you know what a JAR is?"

What I didn't anticipate at that time was how that one question would completely change our discussions over the ensuing months and years. I learned that the game of Minecraft is written in Java, and that my son had been installing mods, which are other JARs, to modify the gameplay. After helping him fix the configuration problem, my son expressed a desire to write a mod and we started exploring how to do that. This marked the beginning of an extremely rewarding and enjoyable journey for the both of us: he taught me about Minecraft, and I taught him basic Java programming concepts. Notes were exchanged over breakfast and dinner, during drives to school or classes while grocery shopping, and pretty much everywhere.

After building our first mod during Christmas 2012, we decided to share the knowledge with his Minecraft buddies. That gave rise to the first Minecraft modding workshop in our living room with about 12 kids. Most of the kids had no programming experience, let alone experience with Java. However, there was high Minecraft experience in the group, with some kids playing for about two years and up to two hours every day. When given the topic of Minecraft, the small group would talk excitedly about different aspects of the game, constantly using hundreds of game-specific terms and phrases as if speaking a different language. My goal was to leverage their passion and introduce them to Java programming.

We built our first trivial mod, but there were a lot of hiccups. After that, everything slowly started to get better. Once we learned more about modding and gained more experience, we were able to improve the quality of the workshops. Since then, my son and I have delivered multiple modding workshops in different cities around the world. Starting a US chapter of Devoxx4Kids in December 2013 (*http:// devoxx4kids.org/usa/*) definitely exploded the interest in and visibility of these workshops, as well as other technology-related workshops targeted toward kids. You can read more about Devoxx4Kids in Appendix D.

Parents whose kids play Minecraft are well aware of how addicting the game can become. Playing the game is a lot of fun, but what makes it more engaging, entertaining, and educational is when kids start building mods. This book is targeted at parents and kids who would like to learn how to mod the game of Minecraft. It can be read by parents or kids independently, but it is more fun to read it together. No prior programming experience is required, but some familiarity with software installation will be very helpful (you'll also need some basic troubleshooting know-how in case there is a problem with the installation, but this information can easily be found via a quick Google search).

How to Use This Book

This book does not intend to teach the game of Minecraft, as that is a vast topic by itself. Refer to the numerous articles at the official Minecraft wiki (*http://mine craft.gamepedia.com/Minecraft_Wiki*) or check out YouTube for tutorials. Appendix A provides a basic introduction to Minecraft for readers who have never played the game.

Chapter 1 starts with a quick overview of the tools required for modding, and provides step-by-step instructions on how to download and install them. The remainder of the chapter walks through how to verify the sample mod bundled in the downloads. We explain the key concepts of the modding tools and familiarize you with Minecraft Forge terminology. This chapter builds the fundamentals required to create mods in subsequent chapters. As with learning any new skill, the concepts covered in this first chapter might be overwhelming for some readers, but it will soon become more familiar.

Moving on from there, Chapters 2 through 5 will walk you through building mods that modify existing parts of the game, such as exploding minecarts, bigger TNT explosions, bouncy sponges, and zombie knights. Each of these chapters has a specific theme: block-break messages (Chapter 2), explosions (Chapter 3), entities (Chapter 4), and movement (Chapter 5). Some of the mods also have variations that you can try out.

Next, we'll explain how to add features to the game such as new commands (Chapter 6), blocks (Chapter 7), items (Chapter 8), and recipes and textures (Chapter 9). This book shows multiple mods that you can build with Forge. Each chapter provides suggestions on what additional mods can be tried based upon what you've learned so far. You are encouraged to try them out.

Once you have them set up, you'll want to share these mods with your friends, so we take a look at how to do that in Chapter 10.

Throughout the book, you will also be exposed to many Java concepts, including keywords and syntax, classes, methods, annotations, control structures, arrays, and much more. Eclipse tooling is used to author Java files, so you'll pick up that skill as well.

The book is focused on learning, so you should find the instructions easy to follow.

Conventions Used in This Book

The following typographical conventions are used in this book:

Italic
: Indicates new terms, URLs, email addresses, filenames, and file extensions.

`Constant width`
: Used for program listings, as well as within paragraphs to refer to program elements such as variable or function names, databases, data types, environment variables, statements, and keywords.

`Constant width bold`
: Shows commands or other text that should be typed literally by the user.

`Constant width italic`
: Shows text that should be replaced with user-supplied values or by values determined by context.

 This element signifies a tip or suggestion.

 This element signifies a general note.

 This element indicates a warning or caution.

Using Code Examples

Supplemental material (code examples, exercises, etc.) is available for download at *https://github.com/AdityaGupta1/minecraft-modding-book*; see Appendix C for download details.

This book is here to help you get your job done. In general, if example code is offered with this book, you may use it in your programs and documentation. You do not need to contact us for permission unless you're reproducing a significant portion of the code. For example, writing a program that uses several chunks of code from this book does not require permission. Selling or distributing a CD-ROM of examples from O'Reilly books does require permission. Answering a question by citing this book and quoting example code does not require permission. Incorporating a significant amount of example code from this book into your product's documentation does require permission.

We appreciate, but do not require, attribution. An attribution usually includes the title, author, publisher, and ISBN. For example: "*Minecraft Modding with Forge* by Arun Gupta and Aditya Gupta (O'Reilly). Copyright 2015 Arun Gupta and Aditya Gupta, 978-1-491-91889-0."

If you feel your use of code examples falls outside fair use or the permission given above, feel free to contact us at *permissions@oreilly.com*.

Safari® Books Online

Safari Books Online is an on-demand digital library that delivers expert content in both book and video form from the world's leading authors in technology and business.

Technology professionals, software developers, web designers, and business and creative professionals use Safari Books Online as their primary resource for research, problem solving, learning, and certification training.

Safari Books Online offers a range of plans and pricing for enterprise, government, education, and individuals.

Members have access to thousands of books, training videos, and prepublication manuscripts in one fully searchable database from publishers like O'Reilly Media, Prentice Hall Professional, Addison-Wesley Professional, Microsoft Press, Sams, Que, Peachpit Press, Focal Press, Cisco Press, John Wiley & Sons, Syngress, Morgan Kaufmann, IBM Redbooks, Packt, Adobe Press, FT Press, Apress, Manning, New Riders, McGraw-Hill, Jones & Bartlett, Course Technology, and hundreds more. For more information about Safari Books Online, please visit us online.

How to Contact Us

Please address comments and questions concerning this book to the publisher:

O'Reilly Media, Inc.
1005 Gravenstein Highway North
Sebastopol, CA 95472
800-998-9938 (in the United States or Canada)
707-829-0515 (international or local)
707-829-0104 (fax)

We have a web page for this book, where we list errata, examples, and any additional information. You can access this page at *http://bit.ly/minecraft-modding-forge*.

To comment or ask technical questions about this book, send email to *bookquestions@oreilly.com*.

For more information about our books, courses, conferences, and news, see our website at *http://www.oreilly.com*.

Find us on Facebook: *http://facebook.com/oreilly*

Follow us on Twitter: *http://twitter.com/oreillymedia*

Watch us on YouTube: *http://www.youtube.com/oreillymedia*

Acknowledgments

We would like to express our gratitude to many people who made writing this book an extremely joyful experience.

First and foremost, many thanks to O'Reilly for providing an opportunity to write this book. The team provided excellent support throughout the editing, reviewing, proofreading, and publishing processes.

At O'Reilly, Brian Foster provided excellent editorial help throughout all the stages of the book. Brian MacDonald, the developmental editor, was always thorough and provided excellent and detailed feedback. Minecraft advice and information was provided to Brian by Alex MacDonald, a seventh grader at Lionville Middle School. Brian and Alex helped to make sure that the level of detail was appropriate for the intended audience, which was of utmost importance to us.

The Tools team at O'Reilly was very helpful in answering all authoring and formatting questions. Jasmine Kwityn's copyedit and Kristen Brown's work as production editor made the book fluent and consistent. Thanks also to the rest of the O'Reilly team, some of whom we may not have interacted with directly, but who helped in many other ways.

Jack Walker, a sophomore at The Dinoff School in Griffin, Georgia, and Adam Cameron Little, an eighth-grader from Consett Academy, Consett, County Durham, United Kingdom, did an excellent technical review and helped shape the book so that it's easy for beginners to start modding.

This book also forms the basis of the Minecraft modding workshops delivered at different worldwide chapters of Devoxx4Kids. Most of our Minecraft modding experience has come from preparing instructions for these workshops. A huge thanks goes to all the instructors, volunteers, and attendees of these workshops over the past months.

Many thanks to Stephan Janssen, a good friend, the man behind Devoxx4Kids, and the author of Appendix D, which provides more information on Devoxx4Kids. May his positive energy and support keep inspiring kids to stay engaged in technology.

The members of the Minecraft Forge Forums were very patient and extremely helpful in answering our questions. We highly encourage you to ask any of your Forge-related questions there.

Last, but not least, we seek forgiveness from all those who have helped us over the past few months and whose names we have failed to mention.

CHAPTER 1

Introduction

Minecraft is a 3D game that involves breaking and placing *blocks* to obtain *materials*. These materials can then be used to build or craft new *items* and *tools*. These, in turn, can be used to harvest more types of blocks. The game also contains *entities*, which are dynamic moving objects in Minecraft (e.g., cows, pigs, and horses). Entities that are hostile are called *monsters* (e.g., zombies and creepers). *Bosses* are monsters that are very hard to defeat. Appendix A provides more details on how to get started with the game of Minecraft.

Playing the game itself is a lot of fun, but the game is even more interesting and engaging because it allows *modifications* (commonly referred to as *mods* in the gaming community). These modifications can change certain aspects of how the game was originally written (e.g., changing the size of a TNT explosion). In addition, they can add content to the game to alter gameplay (e.g., new blocks, items, and smelting recipes).

An individual player uses a *client*, analogous to a program downloaded on your machine. The client by itself is not of much use, though. It connects to a *server*, which is similar to a program running on your machine or a different machine on the Internet. This is called *singleplayer mode*. Minecraft also allows multiple players to join a server. This is called *multiplayer mode*. It's unusual to run a server on your own machine. However, this book will explain how to make mods and run them on your Minecraft client and a server running on your machine.

It is very common to play Minecraft with multiple mods, and there are many kinds of mods that can be made to make Minecraft a more interesting game. The ability to write these mods gives a player complete control over the game. There is no official way to create mods, but there are several third-party vendors that provide that ability; Minecraft Forge is one of these ways.

Downloading and Installing Tools

In order to create mods, we need to use the following tools:

- Java Development Kit
- Minecraft Forge
- Eclipse

Let's learn about these tools and review how to download and install them.

 You can also follow along with a video of the installation instructions on YouTube (*http://bit.ly/1BqmQ2Z*).

Java

Markus "Notch" Persson (*@notch* (*http://twitter.com/notch*) on Twitter) wrote the game of Minecraft using the Java programming language. Java is one of the most popular programming languages. Game developers like Notch write computer programs as text files following the rules defined by Java. Image files end with different extensions like *.png*, *.gif*, or *.jpg*. Movie files end with extensions like *.mov*, *.mp4*, or *.ogg*. Similarly, Java programs are text files ending with the *.java* extension. These text files are called Java *source* files.

Java programs are written as text, but computers understand the binary language of 0s and 1s. To translate the text into something computers can understand, the files must be *compiled*, which is a task done in several steps in Java. The *Java Development Kit (JDK)* is a free toolkit bundled with Java; it is like a Swiss Army knife for Java that provides a variety of tools. The most common tools include the following:

javac
> The *Java compiler* takes the *.java* source file, checks if the class is following the syntax correctly, and converts it into a binary *.class* file. If there are syntax errors, those errors are reported by the tool and the *.class* file is not generated. This process of conversion from source file to binary file in Java terminology is called *compilation*.

java
> The *Java virtual machine (JVM)* reads a *.class* file and interprets it as binary instructions for the computer. This process of reading a binary file and running on the JVM is called *interpretation*.

jar

Used to create or extract a named archive by bundling multiple *.class* files and other files such as images and configuration files. The named archive ends with a *.jar* extension.

These tools are simple to use, and most of the time you don't even realize that they are used in the background to do all the work for you. We'll look at this a little bit later in this chapter.

For Minecraft modding, we'll write Java source files. These files are then converted into binary *.class* files and bundled into JAR files using the tools provided by the JDK. Before you can run Minecraft, and later build mods, you need to install the JDK.

To get started with the JDK, go to its download page at Oracle (*http://bit.ly/TEA7iC*) and install it on your computer by following the instructions (*http://bit.ly/1ESTUoY*).

If you are not sure whether the JDK is already installed on your machine, follow the installation instructions on the website. If the JDK is already installed on your computer, reinstalling it will simply update to the latest version, which is the recommended version for this book.

Minecraft Forge

Minecraft Forge is a tool that helps you build mods. Forge is currently the most popular way to modify the game. Other mod-building tools, such as Bukkit or Mod-Loader, have either shut down or become obsolete.

To get started with Forge, go to the Minecraft Forge downloads page (*http://files.mine craftforge.net/*). As shown in Figure 1-1, you will need to select the version of Minecraft to download.

Select Minecraft Version: All ▼

Figure 1-1. Choosing Forge version

From the drop-down menu, select 1.8. The page should now look like the one shown in Figure 1-2.

 The latest version of Forge at the time of writing this book is 1.8. This version might change by the time this book is published or you are reading this book. So select the appropriate version accordingly. The mods in this book have been made for Forge 1.8. If the mods in this book do not work with future versions of Forge, then we will update the book, as well as the source code on GitHub. Appendix C includes additional details on the GitHub source code.

Promotions

Promotion	Version	Minecraft	Time	Downloads
1.8-Latest	11.14.1.1337	1.8	03/11/2015 06:50:25 PM	(Changelog) (Installer) * (Installer-Win) * (Src) * (Universal) * (Userdev) *
1.8-Recommended	11.14.1.1334	1.8	03/02/2015 03:14:20 PM	(Changelog) (Installer) * (Installer-Win) * (Src) * (Universal) * (Userdev) *
Latest	11.14.1.1337	1.8	03/11/2015 06:50:25 PM	(Changelog) (Installer) * (Installer-Win) * (Src) * (Universal) * (Userdev) *
Recommended	11.14.1.1334	1.8	03/02/2015 03:14:20 PM	(Changelog) (Installer) * (Installer-Win) * (Src) * (Universal) * (Userdev) *

Figure 1-2. Downloading Forge

The first entry in the list shown in Figure 1-2 is 1.8-Latest. In that row, click the link that says Src, which will lead you to an AdFly page. Wait for five seconds and then click Skip Ad in the upper-right corner to download the ZIP file. This file contains the source code of Forge and will be used for modding.

Note that nothing has been installed yet. In fact, it might be tempting to download the Installer. This file, however, is only used to install Forge libraries on your regular Minecraft launcher so that you can load, not make, mods through it. All you've done so far is downloaded a ZIP file that will be used to generate the source for Minecraft.

Eclipse

Eclipse is an *integrated development environment* (*IDE*). An IDE is a tool that can edit files, package and run those files, and help find and fix the errors within those files. There are many IDEs available for use, but this book will use Eclipse for creating our mods.

We will be using Eclipse mostly to make new files, edit them, and run the game to see if they work. Eclipse is a very important tool, because without it you cannot run the game to test it, even if you can edit the source files with another text editor.

To get started with Eclipse, go to the Eclipse downloads page (*http://www.eclipse.org/downloads/*). Figure 1-3 shows how the page looks on a Windows machine. The drop-down menu in the upper-right corner is set to Windows by default, but you can change it to match your operating system.

Figure 1-3. Downloading Eclipse

Click the appropriate link to download the correct version.

 The version of Eclipse at the time of writing this book is 4.4.1. This version might change by the time this book is published or you are reading this book. It would be fine to download the latest available version of Eclipse.

Installing Eclipse is straightforward: it simply involves unzipping the downloaded file. The Eclipse website provides detailed instructions on the installation process (*https://wiki.eclipse.org/Eclipse/Installation*).

Setting Up Forge in Eclipse

We need to set up Forge in Eclipse before mods can be created. In order to do that, create a new directory on your Desktop and call it *forge*. On Windows, this can be created by pressing the Ctrl and Esc keys together, which brings up a textbox where you can type any command that needs to run. Type cmd and press the Enter key, which will open the Command Prompt in a separate window. On Mac, pressing the Command key and space bar together brings up Spotlight, which allows you to search for different commands on your Mac. Type terminal to open up a Terminal window.

The Windows Command Prompt and Mac's Terminal are prebuilt tools that allow you to see all the directories on your operating system, issue commands to manipulate them, and do lots of other interesting things. For now, we'll focus on navigating to the appropriate directory and creating a new one for Forge.

Type the following series of commands at the Command Prompt or Terminal to create the directory and navigate to it:

```
cd Desktop
mkdir forge
cd forge
```

Next, move the previously downloaded ZIP file to this newly created directory. If you use a Mac, double-click the file to extract it in this directory. If you use Windows, right-click the ZIP file, select Extract All, and select this directory to extract the contents. This should create a new *forge/* directory. Change to that directory by using the cd forge command.

Use the dir command on a Windows computer or ls on a Mac computer to see the contents of the directory you are currently in. If you don't see something similar to Figure 1-4, then move on to the next folder and try using dir or ls there, and see if it matches Figure 1-4.

```
03/16/2015  07:46 PM    <DIR>          .
03/16/2015  07:46 PM    <DIR>          ..
03/16/2015  07:46 PM             2,308 build.gradle
03/16/2015  07:46 PM             1,225 CREDITS-fml.txt
03/16/2015  07:46 PM    <DIR>          eclipse
03/16/2015  07:46 PM           352,174 forge-1.8-11.14.1.1338-changelog.txt
03/16/2015  07:46 PM    <DIR>          gradle
03/16/2015  07:46 PM             5,080 gradlew
03/16/2015  07:46 PM             2,404 gradlew.bat
03/16/2015  07:46 PM            26,231 LICENSE-fml.txt
03/16/2015  07:46 PM             1,038 MinecraftForge-Credits.txt
03/16/2015  07:46 PM             2,557 MinecraftForge-License.txt
03/16/2015  07:46 PM             1,581 README.txt
03/16/2015  07:46 PM    <DIR>          src
               9 File(s)        394,598 bytes
               5 Dir(s)  807,317,716,992 bytes free
```

Figure 1-4. Forge folder in Command Prompt

Don't worry about all the files that are shown here (we'll explain these in more depth later). Once you see the correct output, run the command shown in Example 1-1 to set up Forge.

Example 1-1. Setting up a Forge workspace

```
gradlew setupDecompWorkspace eclipse
```

On Mac, you may have to give the command as `./gradlew` instead of just `gradlew`.

 Make sure your computer is connected to the Internet before issuing this command.

The command shown in Example 1-1 will download the required files on your computer and prepare the directory for modding. This may take anywhere from 5 to 30 minutes, depending on the speed of your computer and Internet connection. If everything goes well, the following output will be shown:

```
BUILD SUCCESSFUL
```

In most cases, you should see this output. However, if you do not see this message, the command did not succeed. This could happen for several reasons. First, there might be errors in preparing the directory for modding. If that happens, you should wait a few minutes and try the command again. Another option is to consult the instructions on the Minecraft Forge website (*http://bit.ly/1NfDPvn*). The instructions there may not be up to date; they were for 1.6.4 when this book was written. However, the installation for 1.6.4 is the same as the installation for 1.8, so don't worry about the version.

Another occasion when the command may fail is when you receive the following error:

```
Execution failed for task ':deobfuscateJar'.
```

```
> Java heap space
```

This can be fixed by editing *gradlew.bat* on Windows or *gradlew* on Mac. On Windows, you can use Notepad to edit the file. This can be started by typing `notepad` on the Command Prompt and pressing the Enter key. Open the file by navigating to File→Open… and selecting the *gradlew.bat* file from the correct directory.

On Mac, you can use TextEdit to edit the file. This can be started by going to Applications and clicking TextEdit. Open the file by navigating to File→Open… and selecting the *gradlew* file from the correct directory.

In either case, change `DEFAULT_JVM_OPTS=""` to `DEFAULT_JVM_OPTS="-Xmx1024m"`. Once you've done that, save the file and quit the text editor. Rerun the command after making this change.

If that doesn't work, you can check out the Minecraft Forge forum (*http://www.mine craftforge.net/forum/*). You can search existing threads for the information you need, and if nothing turns up, you can post a question of your own.

After the setup is done, open Eclipse by locating the directory where it was installed and double-clicking *eclipse.exe* on Windows or *eclipse* on Mac. Eclipse is a tool that can do general Java editing, and by default, it has no idea that you want to make Minecraft mods. You will have to tell it that you want to, as well as the location of Forge code and where the mods should be stored. All of this information is stored in a *Project* and created for you as part of the command run in Example 1-1.

The project details are stored in a *workspace*, which is basically a directory in which all your project details are stored so you can work with it easily. A workspace can have multiple such projects. After opening Eclipse, you should see a box similar to the one in Figure 1-5.

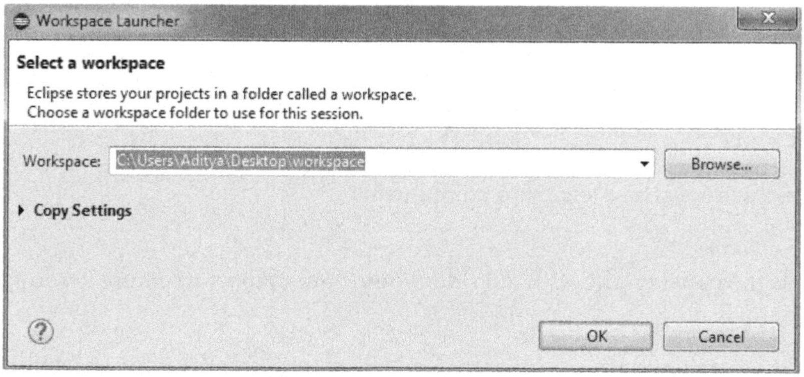

Figure 1-5. Choosing the workspace

Click Browse… to choose the workspace and navigate to the unzipped *forge/* folder. In that folder, there should be another folder called *eclipse/*. Click that folder once to select it, then click Open. Click OK to finalize your choice.

 Make sure to choose the *eclipse/* folder; otherwise, you will not be able to access your project.

If you accidentally clicked OK without choosing the correct workspace location, then quit the Eclipse window and start it again. It will prompt you for the workspace again.

After selecting the correct workspace location in Eclipse, your project will open up, and it should look as shown in Figure 1-6.

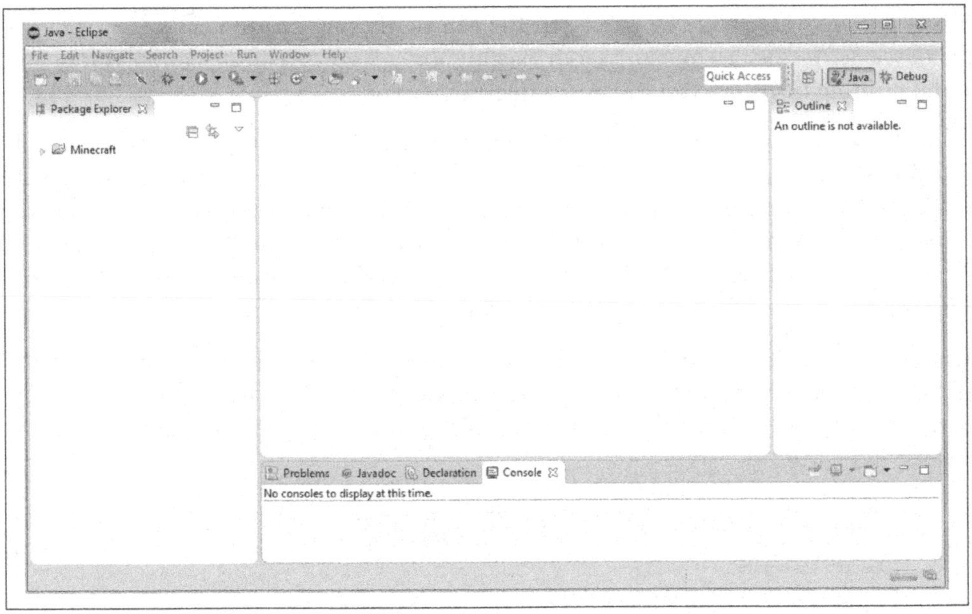

![Eclipse workspace screenshot showing the Java - Eclipse window with menu bar, toolbar, Package Explorer panel on the left containing "Minecraft", a large empty white editing area in the middle, Outline panel on the right showing "An outline is not available.", and Problems/Javadoc/Declaration/Console tabs at the bottom showing "No consoles to display at this time."]

Figure 1-6. Eclipse workspace with project

The Eclipse window has a few main components:

Package Explorer
    This is the panel on the lefthand side, where your project structure is shown.

Big white window in the middle
    This is where your project files are opened and available for editing. Multiple files can be opened in different tabs in this window.

Status window

Located at the bottom of the screen, this window has multiple tabs that indicate the status of different tasks that we perform in Eclipse. For example, the Minecraft server console will be displayed here when we launch the game.

It has a few other windows on the right side, but they are not directly relevant for our modding. Feel free to click **X** to close them.

Understanding the Example Mod

Mods are written as *.java* files, which are later compiled into *.class* files. As mentioned earlier, each Java class is a text-based file, and ends with the *.java* extension. A class follows the set of rules defined by the Java programming language.

In Eclipse, click the arrow next to the *Minecraft/* folder. This expands the folder so that you can see its contents, as shown in Figure 1-7.

```
 ▲ 📁 Minecraft
     ▷ 📦 src/main/java
     ▷ 📦 src/main/resources
     ▷ 📑 JRE System Library [jre8]
     ▷ 📑 Referenced Libraries
     ▷ 📂 build
       📁 common
     ▷ 📂 eclipse
     ▷ 📂 gradle
       📁 jars
       📁 lib
     ▷ 📁 src
       📄 build.gradle
       📄 CREDITS-fml.txt
       📄 forge-1.8-11.14.1.1336-changelog.txt
       📄 gradlew
       📄 gradlew.bat
       📄 LICENSE-fml.txt
       📄 MinecraftForge-Credits.txt
       📄 MinecraftForge-License.txt
       📄 README.txt
```

Figure 1-7. Eclipse workspace with Minecraft project expanded

This expanded folder has many subfolders (identified by another arrow before them) and several files. Most of these are required to create a JAR file for Forge, but fortunately we don't have to worry about all of them. For now, let's see where our mod source files will be added.

Click the arrow next to the *src/main/java* folder. This expands the folder where all the Java source files are stored. Click *com.example.examplemod* to expand a subfolder. It consists of the *ExampleMod.java* Java source file, which is an example mod bundled with Forge. Double-clicking the file shows it in the middle part of the IDE. You can view or make changes to it there.

The Java class looks like Example 1-2.

Example 1-2. Example mod

```
package com.example.examplemod; ❶

import net.minecraft.init.Blocks; ❷
import net.minecraftforge.fml.common.Mod;
import net.minecraftforge.fml.common.Mod.EventHandler;
import net.minecraftforge.fml.common.event.FMLInitializationEvent;

@Mod(modid = ExampleMod.MODID, version = ExampleMod.VERSION) ❸
public class ExampleMod ❹
{
    public static final String MODID = "examplemod"; ❺
    public static final String VERSION = "1.0";

    @EventHandler ❻
    public void init(FMLInitializationEvent event) ❼
    {
        // some example code ❽
        System.out.println("DIRT BLOCK >> "+Blocks.dirt.getUnlocalizedName()); ❾
    }
}
```

There is no need to worry too much about different Java keywords, parentheses, and formatting in this code. However, there are some key Java concepts you should understand:

❶ Each class belongs to a *package*. This is identified using the `package` keyword in Java, followed by a space, the package name, and ending with `;`. This must be the first line in your Java class. It also defines the location of your file (in this case, *com/example/examplemod*).

 Java packages allow logically related classes to be grouped together. This allows similar class names to be used across different packages. This is analogous to sorting different colors of crayons in multiple buckets. Without sorting, it will be difficult to find the appropriate crayon. Similarly, without organizing classes in multiple packages, it will be difficult to find them.

❷ A Java class can use other Java classes from different packages. These classes need to be *imported* so that they can be referred to within the code. Note, however, that this does not mean that the classes are included here, but just that they can be used here. This class is importing four classes.

Each import statement starts with the *import* keyword and provides the fully qualified class name. For example, the `Blocks` class is in the `net.minecraft.init` package, and so is imported as `net.minecraft.init.Blocks`. The `Mod` class is in the `net.minecraftforge.fml.common` package, and so is imported as `net.mine craftforge.fml.common.Mod`. Similarly, other classes are imported from their appropriate package.

❸ `@Mod` tells Forge that this class is a mod and provides some basic information about the mod. The `@` at the beginning indicates that this is a *Java annotation*, which allows Java to define special marks in the code. The exact behavior of this particular annotation is defined by Forge.

A Java annotation can have one or more *elements* that provide more details about the annotation. Each element has a value assigned to it using the equals sign (=). Different elements, along with their value, are separated using a comma.

The `@Mod` annotation has two elements: `modid` and `version`. Their values are defined using `MODID` and `VERSION` *variables* in the class.

❹ Each Java class has a unique name that is followed by the Java keyword `class`. It must match the filename, without the *.java* extension. Our class's name is `Exam pleMod`, so it's saved as *ExampleMod.java*.

The first opening parentheses, {, and the last closing parentheses, }, define the *scope* of the class. This means that everything defined within these two braces belongs to the class.

❺ Defines `MODID` and `VERSION` variables. Variables are used to store values of a specific type. Each variable has a name and a type associated with it. In our case, `MODID` and `VERSION` are the names and `String` is the type, which means they can store text data. Each variable is then assigned a value using = and the exact value is enclosed within quotes. The `MODID` variable has a value of `examplemod`, and the `VERSION` variable has a value of `1.0`.

Java is a case-sensitive language, so make sure the code you make is exactly the same as the code here. For example, if the `S` in `String` was lowercase, you would get an error, because `string` is not a Java class, but `String` is. So `MODID` and `modid` will define two different variables.

❻ Forge mods are created by "listening" for different *events*. Events are something that happens in your world such as initializing a mod, player breaks a block, an entity explodes, a Zombie dies, or a player sends a chat message. An event is handled by an *event handler*. An event handler in a Forge mod is marked with an @EventHandler annotation.

➐ New functionality is added to a Java program by creating new *methods*. A method has four parts:

- *Name* that uniquely identifies the method (init, in our case).
- *Parameters* that provide different functionality based upon their value. Each parameter has a *name* and a *type*. Our method has one parameter with the FMLInitializationEvent type and event name. All the parameters are enclosed between (and), and different parameters are separated by a comma.
- *Body* is the Java code enclosed between { and } that is executed when the method is called. Just as in a class, these parentheses define the scope of the method. This is where all the action that needs to happen is defined.

  The statements inside a method are generally executed from top to bottom, in the order that they appear.
- *Return type* defines a return value that can be used by the caller of this function. If the method returns no value, then a special type of void is used.

  Method init is a special method that is called by Forge when the mod is loaded. This is where the main code for the mod should be defined.

➑ This line is a *comment* in Java and used for giving some useful information to other programmers who are reading the code. Comments can take up one line of the source file and start with two forward slashes, or //. They can also take up many lines, and start with /* and end with */.

➒ Lot of Java concepts are used in this line:

- System.out.println prints messages to the Minecraft server console. It's like calling a method, and the parameters are enclosed between (and).
- The first part "DIRT BLOCK >> " is printed exactly like itself, but without the quotation marks.
- + combines the first string and the value returned by the second method call.
- Blocks.dirt.getUnlocalizedName() returns the name of the dirt block.

The next section reviews the exact message that will be shown in the console.

Running Minecraft and Verifying the Mod

Let's launch the game to see what this mod does!

Press the green arrow shown in Figure 1-8 to run the game.

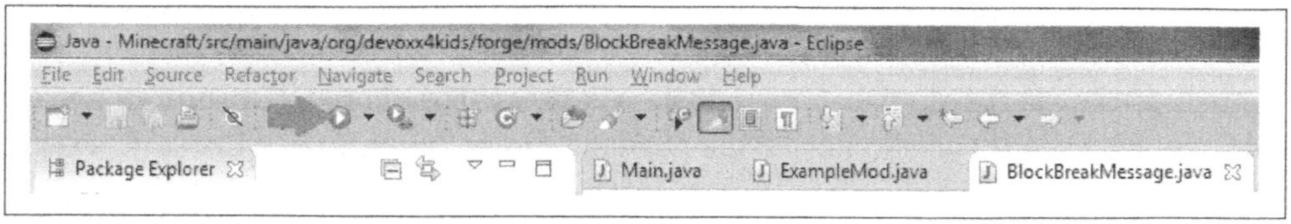

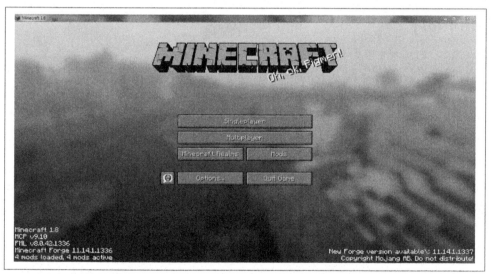

Figure 1-8. Running Minecraft with Eclipse

There is a lot that happens in the background to run the game. Remember `javac`, `java`, and `jar`, all of which are tools that we installed earlier as part of the JDK? Eclipse uses these tools to compile all the Java source files from our project (including the Forge source files and our example mod) into class files. These files are then packaged into a JAR file. This JAR file is then used to run the Minecraft server and the client launcher. The client is also connected to this server as well. This is shown in Figure 1-9.

Figure 1-9. Default Minecraft client

The lower-left corner of the client window shows the version of Forge, 1.8 in this case. It also shows how many mods are loaded, four in this case. Three of the mods are default Forge mods that are required by Forge, and the fourth one is the example mod that is explained in this chapter.

The server console is displayed within a new tab in Eclipse, as shown in Figure 1-10.

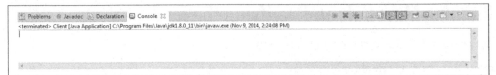

Figure 1-10. Server console in Eclipse

Figure 1-10 shows an empty server console, but this will be populated with messages from the server log. You should see the message shown here in the Minecraft server console:

```
[Client thread/INFO] [STDOUT]: [com.example.examplemod.ExampleMod:init:18]:
DIRT BLOCK >> tile.dirt
```

As the mod is loaded, Forge calls the special `init` method explained earlier. It then executes the code inside this method, which basically prints the game name of the dirt block. You need to scroll up the console to see this exact message, though.

And so now you have run the Minecraft client and can play the usual game. The big difference between now and before is that you can change the game to your liking. Doesn't that feel more exciting than just playing the game?

Summary

Wow, you're already at the end of the first chapter!

This chapter explained how to get started with Minecraft modding using Forge. The tools required for modding were downloaded and installed. The basic structure of the project was opened in Eclipse. A basic introduction to the layout of Eclipse was also introduced. Fundamental Java concepts like class, package, and method were explained while walking through the sample mod. Finally, the Minecraft client was run, and the output from the sample mod was verified.

You are now all set up and ready to create new mods. All the mods in this book mostly follow the same basic pattern as the sample here; you'll just be creating new files and altering them. And you'll see that in action in the next chapter.

CHAPTER 2

Block-Break Message

In the previous chapter, we looked at the sample mod that is bundled with Forge. It printed a message in the console when the game started. However, it is a very simple and boring mod, so in this chapter, we will make one that is slightly more interesting. This mod will send a chat message saying, "You broke a block!" whenever you break a block. This may sound simple, but it will demonstrate some of the fundamental aspects of modding that will be used throughout this book.

Creating the Main File

The most important file in your mods is the *main file*, a Java class. It is also the first file the mod goes to because it has a method that gets called when the game starts. A group of mods will typically have one main file, and this will be the main file for the mods created in this book.

 If you are using a print version of this book, you will obviously not be able to copy and paste the code from it. Instead, follow the instructions in Appendix C to download the source code.

Each Java file needs to exist in a package. The sample mod from Chapter 1 is in the package com.example.examplemod, which makes sense because it is the example mod. For our mods, however, we will be using the package org.devoxx4kids.forge.mods. First, you have to create this package.

In Eclipse, right-click the *src/main/java* folder, and navigate to New→Package, as shown in Figure 2-1.

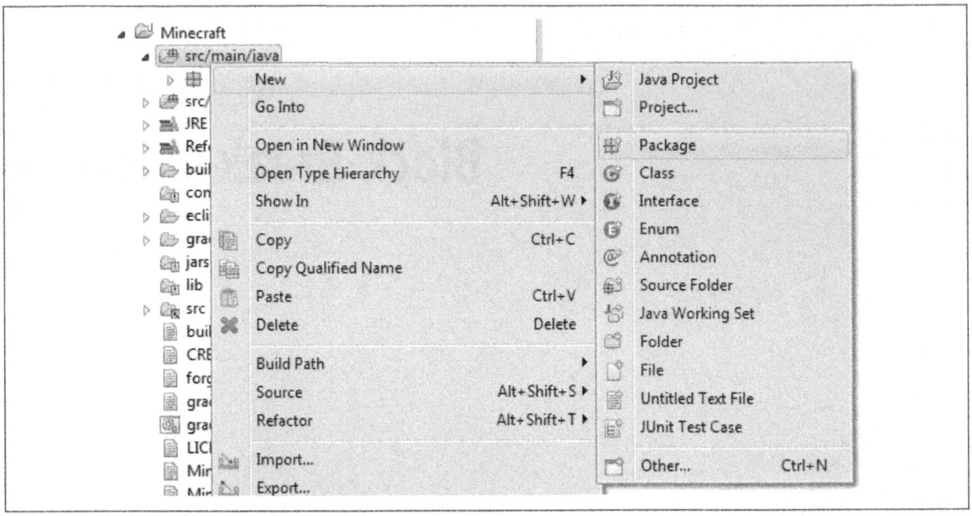

Figure 2-1. Creating a new package

A window asking for the name of the package should open. In the Name box, enter org.devoxx4kids.forge.mods. Don't change any other values. When you are done, it should look like Figure 2-2.

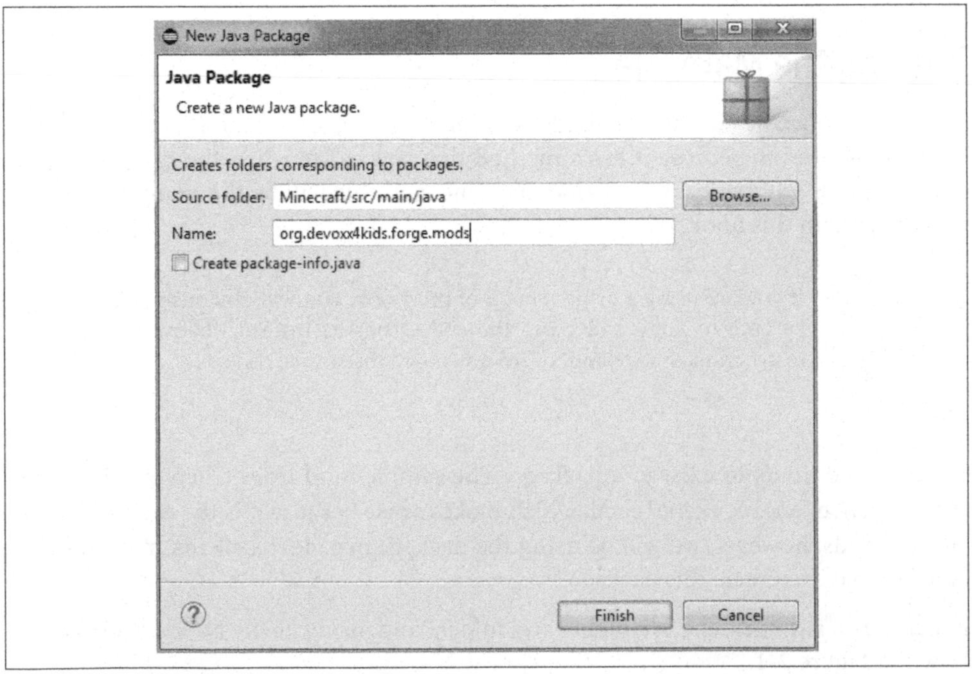

Figure 2-2. Choosing a package name

Click the Finish button to create your package. The directory structure in the Package Explorer should now look like Figure 2-3.

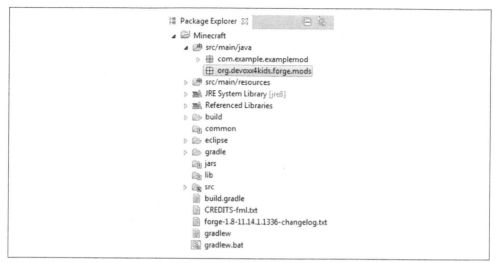

Figure 2-3. Directory structure after new package creation

The package icon is gray right now because you haven't added any Java files to it. Now, you will have to make a main file to register all the event handlers you will make. In Eclipse, right-click your new package and navigate to New→Class, as shown in Figure 2-4.

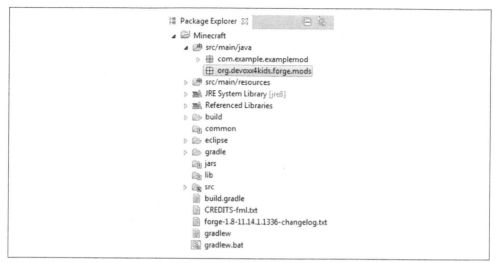

Figure 2-4. Creating the main file

A window asking for the class name should open. In the Name box, enter *Main* (hence the name *main file*). Don't change any other values. The box should now look like Figure 2-5.

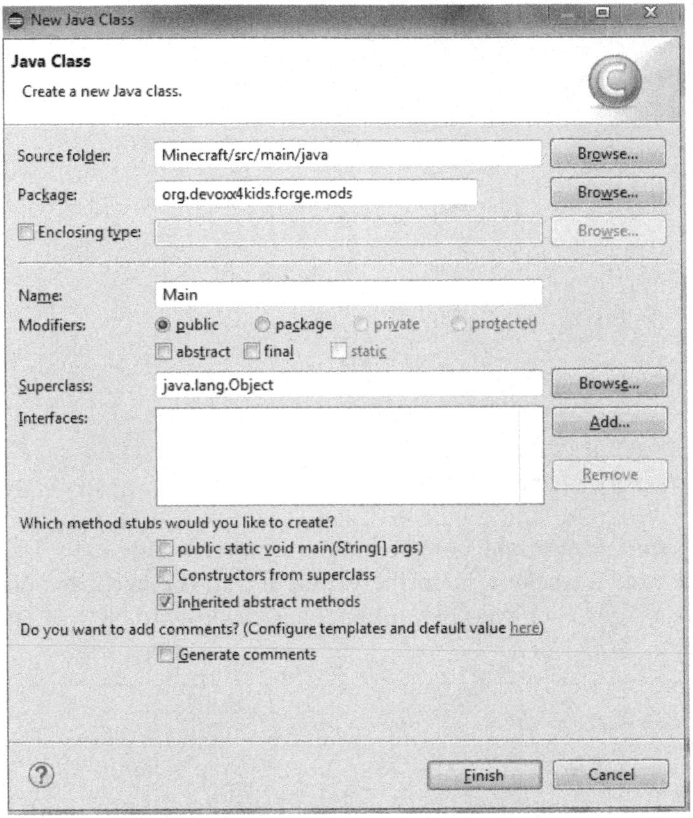

Figure 2-5. Choosing the main file name

Click Finish to create the new file. The directory structure should now look like Figure 2-6.

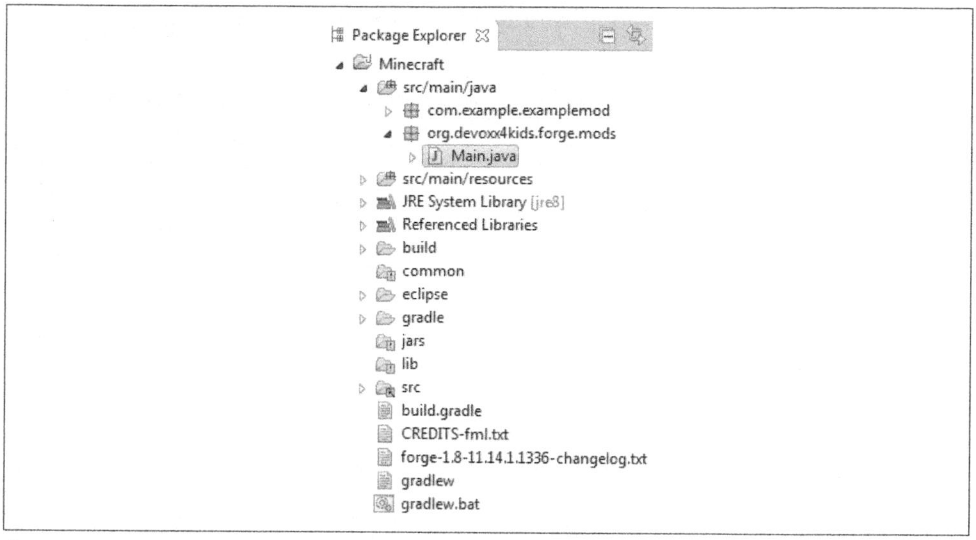

Figure 2-6. Directory structure after main file creation

The package icon should now be brown, because it contains the main file. The work area should show the generated source file, and the source code should look like Example 2-1.

Example 2-1. Main file in the work area

```
package org.devoxx4kids.forge.mods;

public class Main {

}
```

This file looks very small compared to the file for the previous mod, but that is because you haven't added any code to it yet. This file is just a standard starting point for a Java file.

We'll manipulate this file and add some code to it now. First, you will have to add two variables. The first will be the mod's unique identifier, which separates it from other mods. The second will be the version. For now, let's use a fixed value for the version. This value can be updated if a newer version of the mod is created. These variables should be added directly after the line that says `public class Main {`:

```
public static final String MODID = "myMods";
public static final String VERSION = "1.0";
```

The variables are just like the ones in the previous mod, but we've changed `MODID` so that Forge knows this is a separate mod from the example mod. The version is 1.0

because you just created the mod; you can increase it as you go along, but it is not neccessary.

Next, just as with the previous mod, you will need an @Mod annotation. It should look as follows (add it directly before the line that says public class Main {):

```
@Mod(modid = Main.MODID, version = Main.VERSION)
```

The completed class is shown at the end of each section in case you need to better understand where the code should be added.

If you recall, @Mod is an annotation defined by Forge, and it tells Forge that this Java class is the mod's main file. However, you will see an error on the left of the line, and it should look like . This symbol is shown by Eclipse. Whenever this symbol is shown, it means that there is something wrong with your code. In this case, you are using the @Mod annotation but have not imported it yet.

Importing Classes

Press Ctrl-Shift-O on a Windows computer or Cmd-Shift-O on a Mac computer. This will automatically add the code to the file to import the classes from the right package for you.

These *keyboard shortcuts* (or simply *shortcuts*) provide an alternative way to run commands in the menu. A commonly used list of Eclipse shortcuts is shown in "Eclipse Shortcuts" on page 149.

Lastly, you will need to add the initialization method that will run when the game starts. It is shown and should be added after the two variables, but before the last bracket:

```
@EventHandler
public void init(FMLInitializationEvent event)
{

}
```

It looks very similar to the method from the previous mod, but it doesn't have the line that prints out a message with the name of the dirt block. Instead, this method will be used to register the event handlers. The @EventHandler annotation tells Forge to run this method on an event, which in this case is the initialization of the game. The event for this, FMLInitializationEvent event, is shown between the two parentheses. You will see some errors, and again they are related to unimported class files. So import them using Ctrl-Shift-O on Windows or Cmd-Shift-O on Mac. Your main file is now finished, and should look like Example 2-2.

Example 2-2. Finished main file

```
package org.devoxx4kids.forge.mods;

import net.minecraftforge.fml.common.Mod;
import net.minecraftforge.fml.common.Mod.EventHandler;
import net.minecraftforge.fml.common.event.FMLInitializationEvent;

@Mod(modid = Main.MODID, version = Main.VERSION)
public class Main {
    public static final String MODID = "myMods";
    public static final String VERSION = "1.0";

    @EventHandler
    public void init(FMLInitializationEvent event)
    {

    }
}
```

Once you have added the code and imported it, if you still see errors, you probably either misspelled something or forgot to capitalize a letter. As stated in Chapter 1, Java is case sensitive, so make sure that the code you're using exactly matches what is shown here. There should be no errors in your code at this point.

Adding the Event Handler

As explained in Chapter 1, Forge mods are created by *listening* for events. Events happen when something happens in your world (e.g., when a block breaks, an entity explodes, a zombie dies, or a player sends a chat message). Forge can listen for these events and do something when they happen. There is so much that you can do with these events—even simple event-driven mods can be very fun. The Minecraft website includes a complete list of events (*http://bit.ly/1LXnnVu*) for your reference.

Each event handler is basically a method in a Java class that "handles" an event, or performs the intended action when that event occurs (e.g., displaying a chat message when a player breaks a block). Forge lets you write mods that contain multiple event handlers.

Forge provides *event buses* where these event handlers are registered. A good way to visualize what this means is to think of a tour bus in a big city. People get on the bus at one point; then the bus starts going to different places. When the bus reaches a bus stop, some people might go outside to see a tourist spot, but some people might stay inside. After the people see the sights near a particular bus stop, they get back on the bus. The bus goes to multiple bus stops and eventually gets back to its starting point. At that point, all of the people get off the bus and go back to their houses. The next day, it happens all over again. Forge events and event buses operate in the same way. The tour bus is the event bus, the bus stops are the event handlers, and the people are the events. Each day is one tick (1/20th of a second) in Minecraft. When an event happens, it boards the event bus. If the bus stops at an event handler that can handle the event, the event gets off the bus, notifies the handler, and gets back on. When the bus finishes its route, which is when the tick is over, all of the events get off and disappear. Then, in the next tick, the same thing happens again with new events.

Three steps are required for an event handler:

1. Create a Java class for event handling.
2. Add methods that handle different events. Each method must meet two criteria:
   a. Take a parameter identifying the event type that needs to be handled.
   b. Annotate with the @SubscribeEvent annotation.
3. Register the event handler on the event bus.

Creating a Java Class for Event Handling

Now that you have finished your main file, it is time to create the event handler class. In Eclipse, right-click your org.devoxx4kids.forge.mods package again and navigate to New→Class. Notice the package name is automatically chosen for you. This time, in the Name box, enter *BlockBreakMessage*. You can choose any name for the class, but it's important to use a name that shows what the event handler does.

Your event handler class should look like Example 2-3.

Example 2-3. Event handler class in the work area

```
package org.devoxx4kids.forge.mods;

public class BlockBreakMessage {

}
```

Adding Methods for Event Handling

Again, this is just a generic Java file. You will need to add some code to it before it does what you want it to do. In our case, it will send a chat message to the player when she breaks a block. The first thing you will need to add is a method that will run on the event of a block being broken. It looks like Example 2-4 and should be added after the first bracket.

Be sure to import all the relevant classes using Ctrl-Shift-O or Cmd-Shift-O.

Example 2-4. Block-break message event handler method

```
@SubscribeEvent
public void sendMessage(BreakEvent event)
{

}
```

Notice the @SubscribeEvent annotation above the method. This annotation comes from Forge. It tells that the method directly underneath is an event handler method, and will run on the occurrence of an event. The parameter BreakEvent event tells Forge that this method will run on a BreakEvent, which happens when a block is broken. The parameter name is event and can be used in the method.

Now, you have to add some code inside the method to make it send a message to the player who broke the block. The code is shown in Example 2-5 and should go between the { and } to define the scope of the sendMessage method. Again, make sure to import everything after you add this code.

Example 2-5. Block-break message method code

```
event ❶
    .getPlayer() ❷
    .addChatComponentMessage( ❸
        new ChatComponentText( ❹
            EnumChatFormatting.GOLD + ❺
        "You broke a block!")); ❻
```

❶ The block-break event is referred to by the parameter name event.

❷ getPlayer() gets the player who broke the block.

❸ addChatComponentMessage() adds a new chat message to that player's chat bar.

❹ new ChatComponentText() makes a chat message using colors and text.

❺ EnumChatFormatting.GOLD adds a gold color, and + tells it to combine with the text directly afterward.

❻ "You broke a block!" is the actual message.

Combined together, all these elements simply put a message in the player's chat bar saying, "You broke a block!" in golden letters.

Your finished event handler class should now look like Example 2-6.

Example 2-6. Block-break message finished event handler

```
package org.devoxx4kids.forge.mods;

import net.minecraft.util.ChatComponentText;
import net.minecraft.util.EnumChatFormatting;
import net.minecraftforge.event.world.BlockEvent.BreakEvent;
import net.minecraftforge.fml.common.eventhandler.SubscribeEvent;

public class BlockBreakMessage {

    @SubscribeEvent
    public void sendMessage(BreakEvent event){
        event.
            getPlayer()
            .addChatMessage(
                new ChatComponentText(
                    EnumChatFormatting.GOLD +
                "You broke a block!"));
    }
}
```

You may not see as many import statements because sometimes Eclipse condenses them all into one line.

Registering the Event Handler on the Event Bus

Finally, go back to the main file. You can do so by double-clicking *MainMod.java* in the Package Explorer. Add the line from Example 2-7 in the `init` method. This line registers the event handler on the bus, and should be added between the two brackets after `public void init(FMLInitializationEvent event)`.

Example 2-7. Register the event handler

```
MinecraftForge.EVENT_BUS.register(new BlockBreakMessage());
```

`MinecraftForge.EVENT_BUS` is the event bus where all Forge events are registered. There are other buses too, but we won't be using them. The `register` method is called on that bus, and the `BlockBreakMessage` class name is passed. `new` is a Java keyword and creates a new copy, or *instance* in Java terms, of the class. You will see some more import errors, so make sure to import the classes.

Running Minecraft and Verifying the Mod

Now, you can launch the game to test out your mod. Click the green arrow shown in Figure 1-8 to run the game. Chapter 1 explained the background processes necessary to run the game. The only difference here is that the newly added mods are now included as part of compilation and packaging.

Eclipse will ask if you want to save your files. The files need to be saved, or else none of your changes will be included in the compilation. Click OK to save the files and run the launcher. The save file window should look like Figure 2-7.

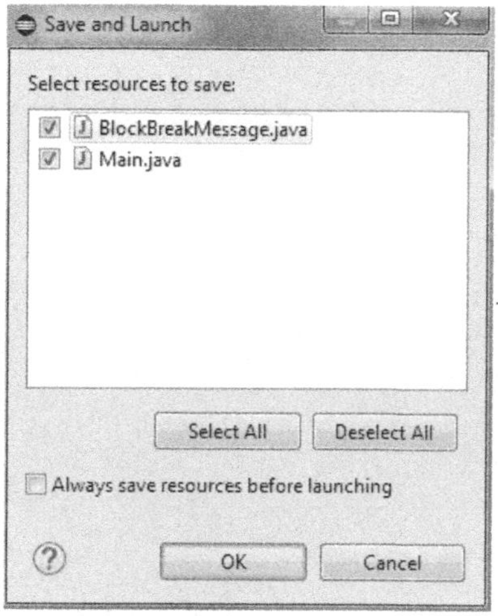

![Save and Launch dialog window with "Select resources to save:" showing checked BlockBreakMessage.java and Main.java, Select All and Deselect All buttons, an "Always save resources before launching" checkbox, and OK and Cancel buttons]

Figure 2-7. Save file window when running Minecraft

Once you have launched Minecraft, make a new world to test your mods. Try to break a block, and you should get a message like the one in Figure 2-8.

Figure 2-8. Message shown when you break a block

Summary

Congratulations, you wrote your very first mod!

This chapter explained how Forge event handlers and the event bus work together to modify the game's behavior. A new event handler class with methods that listen for events was created. A main file was also created, and the event handler class was registered on the event bus there. Basic Eclipse tricks to import Java classes using shortcuts were also used. Fundamental Java concepts like *new* and *instance* were explained while walking through the code. Finally, the Minecraft client was run, and the output from the mod was verified.

Now you know how to listen for events and output a message when that event happens. For instance, `LivingDeathEvent` happens when an entity dies, and if you wanted to, you could print a message when that event occurs. Some other examples of events include `ItemTossEvent` (when a player throws an item), `LivingJumpEvent` (when an entity jumps), and `MinecartCollisionEvent` (when a minecart collides with something). The next couple of chapters will show you samples of other interesting and cool event handlers.

CHAPTER 3

Fun with Explosions

Chapter 2 explained how to make your first mod. Now that the basic fundamentals are well understood, we can move at a slightly faster pace and make more interesting mods. This chapter will teach you how to make mods related to explosions.

First, you will make minecarts explode when they collide with a mob. Next, you will make anvils explode when they fall on an entity. Then, you will make diamond ore explode when mined. Lastly, you will increase the size of TNT explosions. Each mod will also include ways to use the mod, such as falling anvil traps or bouncing zombie towers!

Let's make some explosions!

Exploding Minecarts

Minecarts are one of the main ways of transport in Minecraft. They use rails to travel and can carry mobs or players. However, they don't do much besides that. This mod aims to make our minecarts do some fun stuff. With this mod, minecarts will make a small explosion when they collide with an entity, possibly killing the entity in question.

As explained in the last chapter, a group of mods need to have only one main file. We already created that, and so the only new file that needs to be created is an event handler. Create the event handler as explained in "Creating a Java Class for Event Handling" on page 22, and name it ExplodingMinecarts. Once again, you can use whatever name you like for the file, but it's best to indicate the mod's purpose in the filename.

Add a Java method to this class that will listen for the event. The code you will need to add is shown in Example 3-1 and should be added in the class's scope (i.e., between { and } for the class).

Example 3-1. Exploding minecarts method code

```
@SubscribeEvent
public void explode(MinecartCollisionEvent event){  ❶
    EntityMinecart minecart = event.minecart;  ❷
    minecart.worldObj.createExplosion(  ❸
        minecart,  ❹
        minecart.posX,  ❺
        minecart.posY,
        minecart.posZ,
        2,  ❻
        false);  ❼
}
```

❶ This method runs on a `MinecartCollisionEvent`, which happens when a minecart crashes into an entity.

❷ A variable called `minecart`, of the Forge-defined type `EntityMinecart`, is created to store the minecart in the event. Each Java class can have different properties that store more details about the class. These property values can be accessed by using `.` notation. In this case, the minecart that caused the event is accessed as `event.minecart`.

❸ `worldObj` defines the world in which the minecart exists. The `createExplosion()` method creates an explosion at the specified coordinates. It takes some other parameters, explained next, that define the nature of the explosion.

Even though all the parameters are on separate lines, they're still within the parentheses, and are all considered to be the parameters of the one method.

❹ This parameter is the source of the explosion, which in this case is the minecart.

❺ This line and the two lines after it tell Forge to create the explosion at the x, y, and z coordinates of the minecart. These coordinates are the exact position of the minecart.

❻ The parameter 2 is the power of the explosion, so it will be two blocks in radius.

❼ The parameter `false` tells Forge that the explosion should not break any blocks; if it was `true`, then blocks would be broken.

If you haven't already, make sure to import everything as explained in the Importing Classes tip.

The class should now look like Example 3-2.

Example 3-2. Exploding minecarts final code

```
package org.devoxx4kids.forge.mods;

import net.minecraft.entity.item.EntityMinecart;
import net.minecraftforge.event.entity.minecart.MinecartCollisionEvent;
import net.minecraftforge.fml.common.eventhandler.SubscribeEvent;

public class ExplodingMinecarts {

    @SubscribeEvent
    public void explode(MinecartCollisionEvent event){
        EntityMinecart minecart = event.minecart;
        minecart.worldObj.createExplosion(
            minecart,
            minecart.posX,
            minecart.posY,
            minecart.posZ,
            2,
            false);
    }
}
```

Finally, you need to register it with the event bus by using the following line:

```
MinecraftForge.EVENT_BUS.register(new ExplodingMinecarts());
```

The only difference between this line and Example 2-7 is the name of the event handler: ExplodingMinecarts instead of BlockBreakMessage. Remember, if you named your file differently, then that name should be used here.

Note that this event handler class is registered along with the previously registered handler. So the completed init method would look like Example 3-3.

Example 3-3. init method after registering ExplodingMinecarts event handler

```
@EventHandler
public void init(FMLInitializationEvent event)
{
    MinecraftForge.EVENT_BUS.register(new BlockBreakMessage());
    MinecraftForge.EVENT_BUS.register(new ExplodingMinecarts());
}
```

The order of event handler registration usually does not matter.

Your mod is now finished, and you can test it out!

Run Minecraft by using the green arrow and place some rails down. Place a minecart on the rails and walk into it. You should cause an explosion, because the minecart is colliding with you. When a minecart is exploding, you won't be able to see the minecart because it is covered up by the explosion.

Figure 3-1 shows a practical use of this mod as a security system.

Figure 3-1. House with security system

The minecart is constantly going around the house, so when a mob steps on to the rails, the minecart will bump into the mob and blow it up.

Another fun use of this mod is a bouncing zombie tower. It is shown in Figure 3-2.

To make a tower like this, place a rail down on the ground. Build a tall glass tower around it, about 20 to 30 blocks high. Place a minecart on the rail. Spawn zombies at the top of the tower, and make sure to give them diamond armor or they will die as soon as they hit the minecart.

To spawn a zombie with diamond armor, use this command:

```
/summon Zombie ~ ~ ~{Equipment:[{},{id:diamond_boots},
{id:diamond_leggings},{id:diamond_chestplate},{id:diamond_helmet}]}''
```

You will need to put it into a command block because it is too long to put in the chat window.

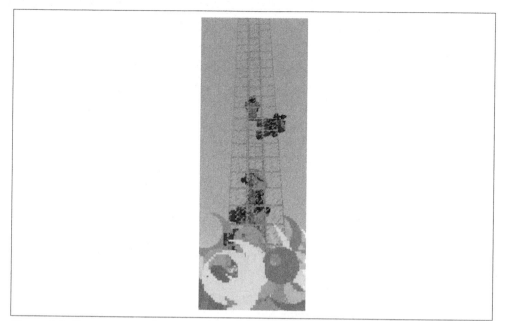

Figure 3-2. Bouncing zombie tower

Exploding Anvils

Now that you have a basic idea of how to create an explosion, we can move on to a slightly more complex mod. This mod will make anvils explode when they fall on an entity. Currently, when anvils fall, they only do damage, but this mod will make them more explosive.

Again, as in the previous mod, the only file you need to create is the event handler file. Its name should be ExplodingAnvils.

The method code you need to add is shown in Example 3-4.

Example 3-4. ExplodingAnvils method code

```
@SubscribeEvent
public void explode(LivingHurtEvent event) { ❶
    if (event.source != DamageSource.anvil) { ❷
        return; ❸
    }

    Entity entity = event.entity; ❹
    event.entity.worldObj.createExplosion( ❺
        entity,
        entity.posX,
        entity.posY,
```

```
        entity.posZ,
        2,
        false);
}
```

❶ This method is run when a living entity is damaged.

❷ This line introduces an important Java concept: the `if` statement. The `if` state-
    ment is used to check whether a condition is true or not. The code within the
    parentheses after `if` is the condition, which in this case is whether the damage
    was caused by an anvil.

    `!=` is a Java *operator*. Operators are used to change a value or compare multiple
    values. Operators like `+`, `-`, and `*` are used to add, subtract, and multiply, respec-
    tively, so they change values. Operators like `==` and `!=` are used to compare val-
    ues. `==` checks whether two values are equal, while `!=` checks whether two values
    are *not* equal. In this case, because the operator is `!=`, the `if` statement runs only
    if the damage source is *not* an anvil.

    Note, `=` is an assignment operator and is different from `==`, which compares two
    values. In this case, we are using neither of them, but it's important to understand
    the difference between the two.

❸ `return` is another important Java keyword. It is used to return to whatever called
    this method (the Minecraft game, in our case).

    In this case, if the damage source isn't an anvil, this event handler ends without
    doing anything, and returns control back to the game.

❹ This line creates a variable of the type `Entity` and the name `entity`, which stores
    the entity that was hurt in the event.

❺ This last line creates the explosion by using the `entity` variable. The method
    parameters are similar to the one explained in Example 3-1.

Make sure to import everything as explained in the Importing Classes tip, if you
haven't already. When importing the `Entity` class, Eclipse will ask you which `Entity`
class you want to import, because there are many to choose from. Choose `net.mine
craft.entity.Entity`. For more help with importing, refer to "Correct Imports" on
page 150.

The final code should now look like Example 3-5.

Example 3-5. Exploding anvils final code

```java
package org.devoxx4kids.forge.mods;

import net.minecraft.entity.Entity;
import net.minecraft.entity.player.EntityPlayer;
import net.minecraft.util.DamageSource;
import net.minecraftforge.event.entity.living.LivingHurtEvent;
import net.minecraftforge.fml.common.eventhandler.SubscribeEvent;

public class ExplodingAnvils {

    @SubscribeEvent
    public void explode(LivingHurtEvent event) {
        if (event.source != DamageSource.anvil) {
            return;
        }

        Entity entity = event.entity;
        event.entity.worldObj.createExplosion(
            entity,
            entity.posX,
            entity.posY,
            entity.posZ,
            2,
            false);
    }

}
```

Register your event handler class with the event bus, as shown here:

```java
MinecraftForge.EVENT_BUS.register(new ExplodingAnvils());
```

Now, you can run Minecraft and try out your code. Spawn an entity such as a creeper or a spider, preferrably in a cage, and build a tower high over it. Place an anvil on the tower so there are no blocks underneath it and it is directly above the spawned entity. The anvil will drop onto the entity and create an explosion. A contraption like the one in Figure 3-3 can automate the process for you.

The anvil is on top of an iron block, which will be pulled back by the sticky piston when the lever is pulled. The anvil will then drop and either kill or greatly damage the villager underneath. The villager will be killed only if the anvil is high enough. The anvil falling already inflicts damage; the explosion just does more damage.

Another example of a use for this mod is an anvil trap. This trap drops an anvil on whoever walks underneath, and it explodes. It looks like Figure 3-4. There is some hidden redstone behind the top redstone torch that powers the sticky piston.

Figure 3-3. Automatic anvil dropper

Figure 3-4. Exploding anvil trap

When a mob steps on the iron pressure plate, the piston above retracts, letting the anvil fall on the unlucky mob's head. However, because the anvil drops from a low position, it won't kill most mobs. If you want to inflict more damage, add more anvils on top of the first one.

Diamond Ore Trap

With this explosive mod, you can make traps with diamond ore as bait. This mod will make diamond ore explode when mined, with an explosion 2.5× as big as a TNT explosion.

First, like any other mod, create the event handler file and call it DiamondOreTrap. The code you need to add is shown in Example 3-6.

Example 3-6. Diamond ore trap method code

```
@SubscribeEvent
public void explode(BreakEvent event) { ❶
        if (event.block != Blocks.diamond_ore) { ❷
                return;
        }

        event.world.createExplosion(null, ❸
                        event.x, event.y, event.z,
                        10, true);
}
```

❶ This method runs on a **BreakEvent**, which happens when a block is broken.

❷ This **if** statement checks whether the block being broken is a diamond ore block. If it is not, the method returns.

❸ This line creates an explosion with **null** as the source. **null** is a Java keyword that basically means "nothing." The explosion is located at the x, y, and z position of the event/block broken, the power is 10, and it does break blocks.

Make sure to import everything. The final code should now look like Example 3-7.

Example 3-7. Diamond ore trap final code

```
package org.devoxx4kids.forge.mods;

import java.util.Random;

import net.minecraft.init.Blocks;
import net.minecraftforge.event.world.BlockEvent.BreakEvent;
import net.minecraftforge.fml.common.eventhandler.SubscribeEvent;

public class DiamondOreTrap {
```

```
@SubscribeEvent
public void explode(BreakEvent event) {
        if (event.block != Blocks.diamond_ore) {
                return;
        }

        event.world.createExplosion(null,
                event.x, event.y, event.z,
                10, true);
}
}
```

Register your event handler class with the event bus, as shown here:

```
MinecraftForge.EVENT_BUS.register(new DiamondOreTrap());
```

Now your mod is done, and you can test it out in Minecraft. One example of a use for this mod is shown in Figure 3-5.

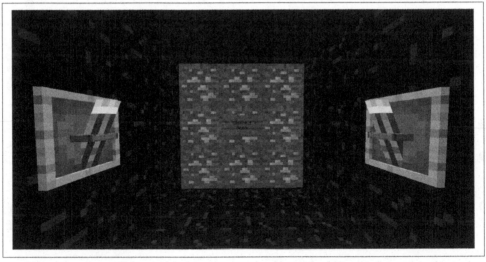

Figure 3-5. Diamond ore trap

A great use of this mod is to save your diamond ore. When players see the diamond ore, they will want to steal it, but when they do, it will explode and kill them!

This mod is also good if you want a bigger alternative to TNT in creative mode. Because it will explode right away, you also don't need to wait for a TNT fuse to burn.

Another way to use the mod is to make a huge bomb. One example is shown in Figure 3-6.

Figure 3-6. Diamond ore trap TNT bomb

The bomb is basically a 5×5×5 cube of TNT with a diamond ore in the middle, and an opening so that you can break the diamond ore. The stairs lead to the platform from which you can reach the ore. The crater made by breaking the diamond ore is shown in Figure 3-7.

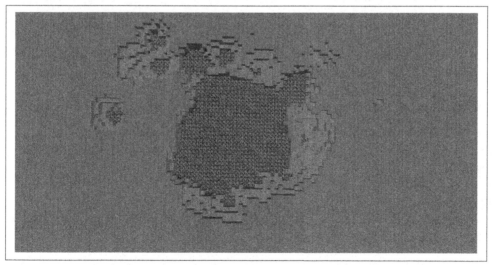

Figure 3-7. Diamond ore trap TNT bomb crater

Bigger TNT Explosions

Currently, TNT explosions are four blocks in radius. This mod will aim to change that by increasing the size. The maximum explosion size allowed by Minecraft is 16 blocks in radius, and we will go all the way up to the limit.

This mod will contain two parts: a simple one and an advanced one. The simple one will make the explosions bigger, but the explosions will happen right away instead of after a fuse of four seconds. The advanced one will contain slightly more code, but it will have a fuse.

First, create an event handler file and call it `BiggerTNTExplosions`. Register your event handler class with the event bus in the main file, as shown here:

```
MinecraftForge.EVENT_BUS.register(new BiggerTNTExplosion());
```

Now proceed to either section for an explosion with or without a fuse.

Without a Fuse

Open `BiggerTNTExplosion` again in the work area. First, you will need to add a variable, right after the first bracket. It should look as shown here and will be used to determine the power of the explosion:

```
float power = 32.0F;
```

`float` is a variable type that can store decimals. By default (i.e., without `F`), Java defines a decimal number of the type `double`. This type allows much bigger decimal numbers. But we need to store only a rather small number, so we can use a `float`. So we need to tell the compiler that the defined decimal number is a float, and *cast* the number to a float by adding `F` after the number. Adding `f` would have the same effect. There are other types of casting available in Java, but we don't need to worry about it.

You can change the number to whatever you want, but the actual explosion might not be the same radius. This is because each block has blast resistance that slows down explosions that break the block. Some blocks, like obsidian, have so much blast resistance that they stop the explosion altogether. The code you need to add is shown in Example 3-8.

Example 3-8. Bigger TNT explosions without fuse method code

```
@SubscribeEvent
public void explode(EntityJoinWorldEvent event) { ❶
        if (!(event.entity instanceof EntityTNTPrimed)) { ❷
                return;
        }

        Entity entity = event.entity; ❸
        event.entity.worldObj.createExplosion(entity, ❹
                                entity.posX, entity.posY, entity.posZ,
                                power, true);
}
```

❶ This method runs on an `EntityJoinWorldEvent`, which happens when an entity is created.

❷ `instanceof` is another Java keyword that returns `true` if the lefthand side of this keyword is not of the type defined by the righthand side.

`EntityTNTPrimed` is a Forge class that defines a primed TNT. Primed TNT is what you get when you light a TNT block. (`event.entity instanceof Enti tyTNTPrimed`) returns `true` if the entity is primed TNT—so far, so good. But you want the method to return if the entity is *not* TNT, so you use the `!` operator to indicate the opposite of the value inside the parentheses.

❸ A variable called `entity` and of the type `Entity` is created, storing the entity from the event.

❹ An explosion is created, using `entity` as the source and location, and with a power of `power`. The explosion also breaks blocks.

Make sure to import everything.

Launch the game and place down a TNT block. Right-click it with a flint and steel to light it. It should explode immediately. Figure 3-8 shows the crater size of a 32-block explosion. Notice that it is not 32 blocks in radius, because of blast resistance. A regular TNT explosion is about four blocks in radius because there are fewer blocks to resist the explosion.

TNT without a fuse also makes for great traps. If you have a house that uses pressure plates to open doors, you can place TNT under the block holding one of the pressure plates. As soon as someone walks over it, it explodes and that person dies (but note that your house will explode as well).

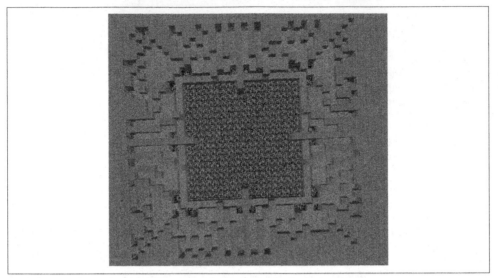

Figure 3-8. Bigger TNT explosions crater

With a Fuse

Open `BiggerTNTExplosion` again in the work area. If you want to make TNT explode with a fuse, it is a good idea to make two variables: one for explosion power and one for the fuse. The variables should look as shown here:

```
int fuse = 4;
float power = 32.0F;
```

"Without a Fuse" on page 38 introduced the decimal variable types `float` and `deci mal`. What if you want to store integers that are whole numbers, and not decimals? Java defines several data types for that, and `int` is the most common type to store such numbers. It can store fairly big integer numbers for our purpose.

Like the explosions without a fuse, you can change the power and fuse to whatever you want. Minecraft uses ticks (1/20th of a second each) as time, but the fuse here is in seconds to make it simpler.

The method code for this mod contains two methods with a lot of code, but it will be broken down into parts to make it easier to understand. It will create an item with four seconds until it despawns. When the item despawns, another event handler will actually create the explosion.

The code is shown in Example 3-9.

Example 3-9. Bigger TNT explosions with fuse method code

```
@SubscribeEvent
public void spawnTNTItem(EntityJoinWorldEvent event) { ❶
        if (!(event.entity instanceof EntityTNTPrimed)) { ❷
                return;
        }

        Entity entity = event.entity; ❸
        EntityItem explosion = new EntityItem(event.world, ❹
                        entity.posX, entity.posY, entity.posZ,
                        new ItemStack(Blocks.tnt));
        explosion.setInfinitePickupDelay(); ❺
        explosion.motionX = 0; ❻
        explosion.motionY = 0;
        explosion.motionZ = 0;
        explosion.lifespan = fuse * 20; ❼
        if (!event.world.isRemote) { ❽
                event.world.spawnEntityInWorld(explosion); ❾
        }
}

@SubscribeEvent
public void explode(ItemExpireEvent event) { ❿
        if (event.entityItem.getEntityItem().getItem() !=
            Item.getItemFromBlock(Blocks.tnt)) { ⓫
                return;
        }

        EntityItem explosion = event.entityItem; ⓬
        event.entity.worldObj.createExplosion(explosion, ⓭
                        explosion.posX, explosion.posY, explosion.posZ,
                        power, true);
}
```

❶ This method runs on an `EntityJoinWorldEvent`, which happens when an entity is created.

❷ Checks whether the item in question is a primed TNT entity; if it isn't, the method returns.

❸ A variable called `entity` and of the type `Entity` is created, storing the entity in the event.

❹ A new `EntityItem` entity called `explosion` is created at the position of the TNT. The item of the entity is set to `new ItemStack(Blocks.tnt)`, which is a block of TNT. `EntityItem` is the entity that is created when an item is dropped.

An ItemStack is a class that stores one stack of items. It contains information like the item type, number of items, and things like enchantments.

❺ This method prevents the item from being picked up, so a player can't disable the TNT by picking up the item.

❻ In this line and the two lines that follow, the motionX, motionY, and motionZ of the item are set to 0, because otherwise, the item would spring up a bit.

❼ The item's lifespan is set to the fuse amount times 20, because it is in ticks, and there are 20 ticks in a second. This will make the item despawn after fuse amount of seconds, triggering the explosion.

❽ An if statement checks if the world isRemote, meaning is it a client world or a server world. In Forge, sometimes events run twice, once on the client side and once on the server side. This if statement contains a line of code that spawns in the explosion item, and it makes sure that only one item is spawned.

❾ This line spawns the explosion item into the world.

❿ This event runs on an ItemExpireEvent, which happens when an item despawns. Because the item created in the previous method despawns when the fuse is finished, this method will run when the fuse is finished.

⓫ event.entityItem.getEntityItem().getItem() returns the item held by the entity. Nothing needs to happen if the item is not TNT, and so != checks whether the item in question is a TNT block; if it isn't, the method returns. event.enti tyItem.getEntityItem().getItem() also shows how properties and methods can be accessed using the . operator.

⓬ Another variable named explosion is used to store the item of the event. Notice that this variable has the same name as the one in the previous method. This is because both the variables were defined in that method's scope. This means they will only exist and be referenced in that method. That way, two or more methods can have a variable with the same name.

⓭ An explosion is created, using explosion as the source and location, and with a power of power. The explosion also breaks blocks.

Make sure to import everything. When importing Item, select net.mine craft.item.Item from the list of options. Refer to "Correct Imports" on page 150 for a complete list of imports.

You are now ready to test out your mod in Minecraft. Just as you did for the explosions without a fuse, place a TNT block and light it with a flint and steel. You might be able to see the item created.

The only time this mod does not work correctly is when the item falls through a hole, but because the TNT is offset a bit when it is lit, it stays on top. Because the item causes the explosion, the big explosion happens at the bottom of the hole, and a small one happens on top because of the primed TNT entity.

Summary

In this chapter, you learned a lot about mods that made explosions. You learned about lots of different events, such as MinecartCollisionEvent, BreakEvent, and EntityJoinWorldEvent. You created mods like explosive minecarts and bigger TNT explosions, both with and without a fuse. Now that you have a better understanding of how to use event handlers, you can use them to make villagers explode when they spawn, enlarge creeper explosions, or make players explode when they get hurt.

The next chapter will be about entities and mobs, and how you can change their behavior.

CHAPTER 4

Entities

Now that you have a good understanding of how to make mods with event handlers, we can move on to other types of mods. The theme of Chapter 3 was explosions, which are fun, but this chapter's theme will be entities. First, you will make pigs drop diamonds in addition to their normal drop of porkchops. Next, you will make all zombies receive diamond armor and a diamond axe when they spawn. Finally, you will allow creepers to spawn five reinforcements when they die.

Pigs Dropping Diamonds

Pigs are passive entities. They will follow you if you hold a carrot. You can also breed them with a carrot. You can even ride on them with a saddle and a carrot on a stick. When pigs die, they drop porkchops. Wouldn't it be fun to make them drop diamonds or some other material instead? Let's do that!

First, create an event handler class called PigsDroppingDiamonds. The method code you need to add is shown in Example 4-1.

Example 4-1. Pigs dropping diamonds method code

```
@SubscribeEvent
public void dropDiamonds(LivingDeathEvent event){ ❶
        if (!(event.entity instanceof EntityPig)) { ❷
                return;
        }

        Random random = new Random(); ❸

        if (!event.entity.worldObj.isRemote) { ❹
                event.entity.dropItem(Items.diamond, random.nextInt(3)); ❺
```

```
        }
}
```

❶ This method runs on a `LivingDeathEvent`, which happens when an entity dies.

❷ If the entity is not a pig, the method returns.

❸ This line creates a new variable of the name `random` and type `Random`. This is a Java class that generates random numbers.

❹ If the world is not a client world, tested by the `isRemote` field, then the method continues. If this statement was not here, the pig would drop twice the number of items, but half of the items would be *ghost items*, and would be impossible to pick up.

❺ `dropItem` is a method on the `entity` class that drops an item at the position of the entity. It takes two parameters: the first is the item to be dropped, and the second is the number of items to be dropped.

In this case, `event.entity` refers to the pig. `Items` is a Forge class that has the complete list of items in Minecraft. `Items.diamond` refers to the diamond item, as the name says. The `nextInt()` method gets a random number between 0 and the number before the parameter given, 2 in this case. This line then drops 0 to 2 diamond items when the pig dies.

The final code should look like Example 4-2.

Example 4-2. Pigs dropping diamonds final code

```
package org.devoxx4kids.forge.mods;

import java.util.Random;

import net.minecraft.entity.passive.EntityPig;
import net.minecraft.init.Items;
import net.minecraftforge.event.entity.living.LivingDeathEvent;
import net.minecraftforge.fml.common.eventhandler.SubscribeEvent;

public class PigsDroppingDiamonds {

        @SubscribeEvent
        public void dropDiamonds(LivingDeathEvent event){
                if (!(event.entity instanceof EntityPig)) {
                        return;
                }

                Random random = new Random();
```

```
            if (!event.entity.worldObj.isRemote) {
                    event.entity.dropItem(Items.diamond, random.nextInt(3));
            }
        }
}
```

Make sure to import everything, and import `java.util.Random` when you are importing the `Random` class.

Now, you are ready to try out your mod.

Run Minecraft by clicking the green arrow at the top and log in to your world. Spawn a pig by using a Spawn Pig item, and kill it by using a sword. You should see something like Figure 4-1.

Figure 4-1. A pig dropping a diamond

There are a variety of items in Minecraft. Instead of dropping diamonds, you can experiment with dropping some other items as well. You are limited, however, to items known to Forge. So delete `diamond` from the code, place your cursor right after `Items.` and press Ctrl-Space. This will show the list of Minecraft items that are known to Forge, as shown in Figure 4-2.

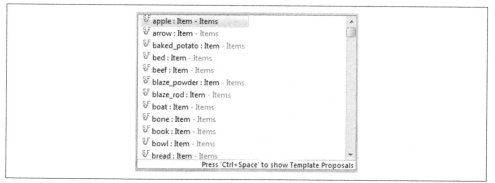

Figure 4-2. List of items in Forge

You can select any item that you wish, click the green arrow to run Minecraft, and your dead pig will then drop that particular item. For example, a pig dropping a potato is shown in Figure 4-3.

Figure 4-3. A pig dropping a potato

The brown splotch under the pig is the potato that it dropped.

Another twist to this mod involves dropping a block, instead of an item, when the pigs die. For example, change `Items.diamond` to `Item.getItemFrom Block(Blocks.cobblestone)` to drop a cobblestone instead of a diamond. You need the `Item.getItemFromBlock()` method because `Blocks.cobblestone` is a block, not an item, so it can't be used in the method `dropItem()`. `Item.getItemFromBlock()` turns it into an `ItemBlock`, which is the item version of the block. A pig dropping a cobblestone is shown in Figure 4-4.

Figure 4-4. A pig dropping a cobblestone

Just as the complete list of items can be seen by placing the cursor after `Items.` and pressing Ctrl-Space, the complete list of blocks can be seen by placing the cursor right after `Blocks.` and using the same key sequence. This is shown in Figure 4-5.

Try dropping different items and blocks when the pig dies.

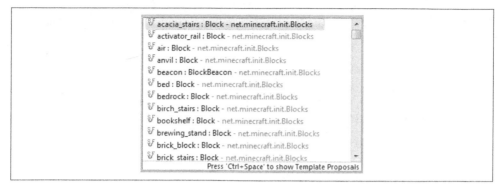

Figure 4-5. List of blocks in Forge

Any living entity such as a cow, iron golem, or skeleton fires a `LivingDeathEvent` as well. Change the first line in the `dropDiamonds()` method to check for that particular entity instead of `EntityPig`. For example, replace `EntityPig` with `EntityIronGolem` to change the items dropped on iron golem death. This will allow you to drop any item or block on the death of that entity.

Zombie Knights

Zombies are the most common hostile mobs in the game. They also drop many things (e.g., iron ingots and carrots), and they can pick up armor. This next mod will make zombies spawn with armor whenever they enter the world. They will also be given an axe. This way, zombies will be much stronger and harder to kill.

First, make an event handler class called `ZombieKnights`. Then, add the code shown in Example 4-3.

Example 4-3. Zombie knights method code

```
@SubscribeEvent
public void giveArmor(EntityJoinWorldEvent event){  ❶
        if (!(event.entity instanceof EntityZombie)) {  ❷
                return;
        }

        EntityZombie zombie = (EntityZombie) event.entity;  ❸

        zombie.setCurrentItemOrArmor(0, new ItemStack(Items.diamond_axe));  ❹
        zombie.setCurrentItemOrArmor(1, new ItemStack(Items.diamond_chestplate));  ❺
        zombie.setCurrentItemOrArmor(2, new ItemStack(Items.diamond_leggings));
        zombie.setCurrentItemOrArmor(3, new ItemStack(Items.diamond_boots));
        zombie.setCurrentItemOrArmor(4, new ItemStack(Items.diamond_helmet));
}
```

❶ This method runs on an `EntityJoinWorldEvent`, which happens when an entity is created.

❷ If the entity is not a zombie, the method returns.

❸ This line shows a good example of *casting* in Java. Before we understand the concept of casting, let's first discuss *inheritance*.

Java allows a class to be *derived* from another class. A class that is derived from another class is called a *subclass* or a *child class*. The class from which the subclass is derived is called a *superclass* or a *parent class*. A child class inherits a parent class by using the `extends` Java keyword. So a child class is also known to *extend* the parent class.

For example, `Animal` could be a parent class, and `Cat`, `Fish`, and `Bat` could be child classes. Each animal knows how to eat, and that ability can be defined in the `Animal` class. However, each animal also has special abilities that separate them from the others (e.g., in our sample of animals, only cats can walk, only fish can swim, and only bats can fly). Those specific abilities can then be defined in their respective child classes.

A class can be derived from a class that is derived from another class, and so on, and ultimately derived from the topmost class, `java.lang.Object`. All the classes up to `java.lang.Object` are said to be in the *parent hierarchy* of the child class. This concept is commonly known as inheritance. A subclass *inherits* fields and methods of all the classes in the parent hierarchy.

Casting is taking an object and "turning it into" an object of a different type. Specifically, you can take an object from the parent hierarchy and cast it into an object of a more specific type.

In our case, `Entity` is in the parent hierarchy of `EntityZombie`. So after we've confirmed that the given entity is of the type `EntityZombie`, as done in ❷, we can cast `event.entity` to `EntityZombie`. This will allow us to call all the methods from `EntityZombie`, of course, after casting. We are particularly looking for methods that give armor/items to the zombie.

Casting is done by specifying the more specific type in parentheses, (and), before the more generic type.

❹ The `setCurrentItemOrArmor` method assigns an item or armor at a particular slot for the given entity. There are five available slots, starting with slot 0. The first slot is meant for an item that the entity will hold. This line gives the zombie a diamond axe in this slot.

❺ The next four slots are meant for armor. This line and the three lines after it give the zombie full diamond armor in the armor slots: 1–4. Slot 1 is chestplate, slot 2 is leggings, slot 3 is boots, and slot 4 is helmet. You can put any kind of these armor in the appropriate slot, and in this mod, all the armor is diamond armor.

Import everything, and you should then be good to go.

The final code should look like Example 4-4.

Example 4-4. Zombie knights final code

```
package org.devoxx4kids.forge.mods;

import net.minecraft.entity.monster.EntityZombie;
import net.minecraft.entity.passive.EntityHorse;
import net.minecraft.init.Items;
import net.minecraft.item.ItemStack;
import net.minecraftforge.event.ServerChatEvent;
import net.minecraftforge.event.entity.EntityJoinWorldEvent;
import net.minecraftforge.event.entity.living.LivingHurtEvent;
import net.minecraftforge.fml.common.eventhandler.SubscribeEvent;

public class ZombieKnights {

    @SubscribeEvent
    public void giveArmor(EntityJoinWorldEvent event){
        if (!(event.entity instanceof EntityZombie)) {
            return;
        }

        EntityZombie zombie = (EntityZombie) event.entity;

        zombie.setCurrentItemOrArmor(0, new ItemStack(Items.diamond_axe));
        zombie.setCurrentItemOrArmor(1, new ItemStack(Items.diamond_chestplate));
        zombie.setCurrentItemOrArmor(2, new ItemStack(Items.diamond_leggings));
        zombie.setCurrentItemOrArmor(3, new ItemStack(Items.diamond_boots));
        zombie.setCurrentItemOrArmor(4, new ItemStack(Items.diamond_helmet));
    }
}
```

Run Minecraft by clicking the green arrow. Spawn a zombie, and it should have a diamond armor.

In Chapter 3, in the bouncing zombie tower picture, all the zombies had full diamond armor. This is because the player who took the screenshot was using the zombie knights and the exploding minecarts mods at the same time. An example of a zombie knight by itself is shown in Figure 4-6.

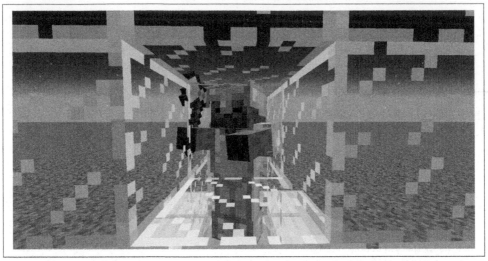

Figure 4-6. Zombie knight

Creeper Reinforcements

The final mod in this chapter will be about creepers. Creepers are probably the most famous hostile mob in Minecraft, even if they aren't the most common one. A bit of interesting history about the creeper: its entity model (shape) was made when Notch accidentally inverted the model of a pig.

This mod will spawn five creepers when a creeper dies, making the game *much* harder. You won't be able to just kill the creepers, but will instead have to trap them. If you make the mistake of killing them, five more will attack you.

Create an event handler class called `CreeperReinforcements`. The method code for it is shown in Example 4-5.

Example 4-5. Creeper reinforcements method code

```
@SubscribeEvent
public void spawnReinforcements(LivingDeathEvent event){ ❶
        if (!(event.entity instanceof EntityCreeper)) { ❷
                return;
        }

        for (int i = 0 ; i < 5 ; i++) { ❸
                EntityCreeper creeper = new EntityCreeper(event.entity.worldObj); ❹
                creeper.setLocationAndAngles(event.entity.posX, ❺
                        event.entity.posY,
                        event.entity.posZ,
                        0,
                        0);
```

```
        if (!event.entity.worldObj.isRemote) { ❻
            event.entity.worldObj.spawnEntityInWorld(creeper); ❼
        }
    }
}
```

❶ This method runs on a `LivingDeathEvent`, which happens when an entity dies.

❷ If the entity is not a creeper, the method returns.

❸ This line is the start of a `for` loop, another Java concept. A `for` loop is a way to repeat code until a certain condition is met. The general form of the `for` loop requires three values between the parentheses: the *initialization*, *termination*, and *increment*. These values are separated by semicolons. The initialization is run once, as the loop begins. The termination tells the loop when to stop; when the statement in this section becomes `false`, the loop stops. This statement is checked after each repetition of the code. The increment happens after each time a loop is completed. The code that is repeated every time is within the opening bracket after `for (int i = 0 ; i < 5 ; i++)` and the corresponding closing bracket two lines after `event.entity.worldObj.spawnEntityInWorld(creeper);`.

In this case, a new integer variable called `i` is made in the initialization and set to `0`. The termination says to keep going until `i` is *not* less than 5. `++` is a new Java operator called an *increment*. This operator can be placed after an integer variable, and increments the value of the variable by 1. In our case, the increment says to increase `i` by 1 each time.

So when the loop starts out, `i` is set to `0` and the code inside the `for` loop is run once. After the completion of the first run, it is incremented by 1, so it is now equal to 1. Before the next run of the loop, the termination condition is checked. If it is `false`, then the loop is stopped and the next Java statement after the loop is executed. If it is `true`, then the loop is run once again, the value incremented, the termination checked, and so on.

This keeps going on until `i` is incremented to 5, at which point it is *not* less than 5, because it is equal to 5. The loop has run five times by now. Because the termination statement is `false`, the loop stops.

❹ A new variable called `creeper` is created. This variable will store the creeper that should be spawned. Because it is inside the `for` loop, it will run five times.

❺ This moves the creeper to the position of the dead creeper. It is also inside the `for` loop.

This `if` statement checks whether the world is remote (`isRemote`). Just as in the bigger TNT explosions mod, this is done so that the statement inside does not run twice. If this statement was not here, five regular creepers would spawn, but five creepers without AI would also spawn. If a mob does not have AI, it can't move and can't take any damage.

❼ This spawns the creeper. Because this line and the surrounding `if` statement are in the `for` loop, they will run twice.

You have now finished your mod and can test it out in Minecraft. Spawn a creeper by using a Spawn Creeper item, and kill it with a diamond sword. Five more creepers should spawn. Figure 4-7 shows what happens if you spawn one creeper and constantly kill its offspring. You can also spawn an iron golem inside the area, and it will start killing creepers and making more for you. When one creeper explodes, a lot of creepers will die and make tons of creepers. The only way to get rid of them is by setting your game difficulty to *peaceful*.

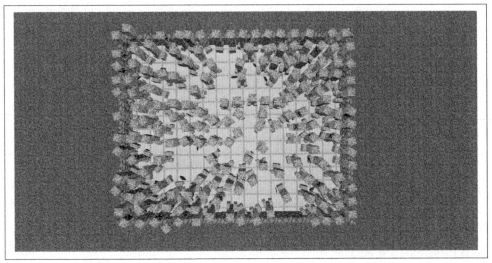

Figure 4-7. Creeper infestation

Notice the gray items in the picture; those are the gunpowder items dropped upon creeper death. There are also a few experience orbs, which are dropped upon a mob's death. All these creepers came from one creeper, which eventually multiplied on death.

Summary

In this chapter, you learned about entities and how you can mod them to make them more interesting. First, you made pigs drop diamonds. You also learned how different items and blocks can be dropped and how the same technique can be applied to other living entities. Armored zombies were created, and finally, you made creepers spawn reinforcements on death. Now that you know how to modify entities' behavior, you can make cool mods like faster creepers, skeletons with swords, and flying pigs.

We discussed Java concepts like generating random numbers, using a `for` loop for repeating code until a condition was met, and using the increment operator. We also looked at inheritance and casting, two fundamental concepts that were applied in multiple places.

In the next chapter, you will learn about movement and how to mod the player's movement.

CHAPTER 5

Movement

Most entities in Minecraft—such as creepers, pigs, and zombies—move in the game. But they don't have the capability to jump or get damaged when they fall. Also, none of the entities except spiders can climb up walls, and spiders can climb only up to three blocks high. In this chapter, you'll learn how to change all this by modding the movement of the player.

First, you will make the player jump much higher; then you will add a parachute so that the player can avoid fall damage. Finally, you will make a mod that lets snow golems and iron golems climb up walls to reach hostile mobs that they can kill.

Super Jump

A Minecraft player can normally jump up to 1.252 blocks. This is typically done to jump over a block or get out of a cave. But what if you were to jump over a cliff that is much higher or a cave that is much deeper? This mod will give you the ability to jump much higher and reach new heights.

First, make a new class and call it SuperJump. Register it in the main file to activate the mod. The event handler method code that needs to be added to this class is shown in Example 5-1.

Example 5-1. Super jump method code

```
@SubscribeEvent
public void makeJumpHigher(LivingJumpEvent event){  ❶
        if (!(event.entity instanceof EntityPlayer)) {  ❷
                return;
        }
```

```
        event.entity.motionY *= 5;  ❸
}
```

❶ This method runs on a LivingJumpEvent, which happens when an entity jumps.

❷ If the entity is not a player, the method returns. It would be kind of weird to see creepers or zombies jumping 10 blocks into the air, so we are limiting this method to only players.

❸ * is an arithmetic operator that multiplies two values. For example, if x and y are two variables, then they can be multiplied using x * y. = is an assignment operator that is used to assign the value on the right side of the operator to the left side. For example, result = x * y will multiply x and y and assign it to the result variable. *= is a combined operator that multiplies the value on the left side by the value on the right side and assigns it back to the left side.

In our case, the player's Y motion is multiplied by 5 and assigned back to itself. So if the motionY field was equal to 2 when the method ran, it would be equal to 10 afterward.

The final code of the event handler should look like Example 5-2.

Example 5-2. Super jump final code

```
package org.devoxx4kids.forge.mods;

import net.minecraft.entity.player.EntityPlayer;
import net.minecraftforge.event.entity.living.LivingEvent.LivingJumpEvent;
import net.minecraftforge.fml.common.eventhandler.SubscribeEvent;

public class SuperJump {

        @SubscribeEvent
        public void makeJumpHigher(LivingJumpEvent event){
                if (!(event.entity instanceof EntityPlayer)) {
                        return;
                }

                event.entity.motionY *= 5;
        }
}
```

An important part to understand is that this only multiplies the Y motion by 5, which does not translate into jumping 5 blocks. Figure 5-1 shows approximately how Y motion multiplication is translated to the jump height in a number of blocks. So if the Y motion is multiplied by 2, then the player jumps by 4.5 blocks. If the Y motion is multiplied by 5, then the player jumps by 23 blocks, and so on.

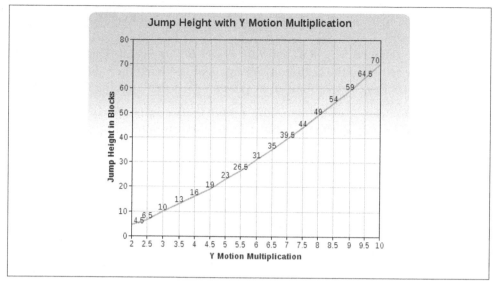

Figure 5-1. Translate Y motion to number of blocks

Now, you are ready to test out your new mod in Minecraft.

Click the green arrow in Eclipse to run Minecraft. Log on to your existing world and try to jump. You should find yourself 23 blocks in the air.

A player in mid-jump is shown in Figure 5-2.

Figure 5-2. Player in mid-jump with super jump mod

We can tell that the player is very high up because the detail on the blocks on the ground is very hard to see.

In a variation to the mod, you don't allow the player to jump at all. This can be done by changing the setting of the Y motion value to 0, or changing the value 5 to 0. This way, you are restricting the Y motion of the player to 0, so that jumping is impossible.

This updated mod can be used by making a maze that's constantly going down one block. Players will not be able to backtrack because they cannot jump.

Bouncy Sponges

If you don't like being able to jump high all the time, you can add some code that lets you do it only when you are standing on a sponge. Add the code shown here after the last bracket of the `if` statement in the regular version:

```
if (event.entity.worldObj.getBlock(
                ((int) Math.floor(event.entity.posX)),
                ((int) Math.floor(event.entity.posY)) - 2,
                ((int) Math.floor(event.entity.posZ))) != Blocks.sponge) {
        return;
}
```

The code checks that the block under you is a sponge. This is done by using the `Math.floor()` method. `Math.floor` is a Java function that rounds a decimal down to the nearest integer value. You can get entity coordinates as a decimal, but a block uses integer coordinates. For example, if a player was standing over a sponge, and the player was at X 526.1, Y 10, and Z 102.42, the sponge would be at X 526, Y 9, and Z 102. However, `Math.floor()` expresses the integer value as a `float`, so the code casts the floored coordinates to `int`.

Notice that the code is checking for the block that is two blocks below the player; this is because when the player jumps, the sponge will be that distance from the player.

The final code should now look like Example 5-3.

Example 5-3. Bouncy sponges final code

```
package org.devoxx4kids.forge.mods;

import net.minecraft.entity.Entity;
import net.minecraft.entity.player.EntityPlayer;
import net.minecraft.init.Blocks;
import net.minecraft.util.ChatComponentText;
import net.minecraftforge.event.entity.living.LivingEvent.LivingJumpEvent;
import net.minecraftforge.fml.common.eventhandler.SubscribeEvent;

public class BouncySponges {
```

```
@SubscribeEvent
public void bounce(LivingJumpEvent event) {
        if (!(event.entity instanceof EntityPlayer)) {
                return;
        }

        if (event.entity.worldObj.getBlock(
                ((int) Math.floor(event.entity.posX)),
                ((int) Math.floor(event.entity.posY)) - 2,
                ((int) Math.floor(event.entity.posZ))) != Blocks.sponge) {
                return;
        }

        event.entity.motionY *= 5;
    }
}
```

Run your Minecraft by clicking the green arrow. Log into your world and place a sponge from your inventory. Try to jump on a nonsponge surface and make sure that you are not able to jump. And now try to jump on a sponge, and check whether you can jump.

As earlier, Figure 5-1 shows how many blocks you will jump based upon the Y motion multiplication.

Parachute

In Minecraft, if you fall more than three blocks higher, then you hurt yourself. Each block over the three-block limit causes more damage with the fall. If you have the super jump mod enabled, you can jump much higher, but that means you'll be at risk of hurting yourself more as well.

This mod will complement the previous mod by adding a parachute that you can use to avoid fall damage from higher jumps. The parachute will be activated by pressing the Shift key, but there will not be any visible changes when you activate a parachute.

First, make a new class and call it `Parachutes`. Add the event handler method code shown in Example 5-4.

Example 5-4. Parachute method code

```
@SubscribeEvent
public void deployParachute(PlayerTickEvent event) { ❶
        EntityPlayer player = event.player; ❷
        if (!player.isAirBorne || !player.isSneaking()) { ❸
                return;
        }

        event.entity.motionY = -0.05; ❹
```

```
}

@SubscribeEvent
public void negateFallDamage(LivingFallEvent event) { ❺
    if (!(event.entity instanceof EntityPlayer)) { ❻
            return;
    }

    EntityPlayer player = (EntityPlayer) event.entity; ❼

     if (!player.isSneaking()) { ❽
            return;
    }

    event.setCanceled(true); ❾
}
```

❶ This method runs on `PlayerTickEvent`, which happens for every player on every tick.

❷ A new variable is made to store the player of the event.

❸ If the player is *not* airborne, or if the player is *not* sneaking, the method returns. This is because the parachute needs to be active only when the player is airborne or sneaking.

   ! is a Java operator that negates the statement between (and). In other words, it tells the `if` statement to run if the statements are *not* true. The || operator is a Java or operator, so the `if` statement will run if either of the statements are true.

❹ The Y motion of the player is set to `-0.05`, which is the same as a slow descent. This number can be from `-0.01` for a really slow descent to `-0.1` for a slightly slower descent.

❺ This method runs on a `LivingFallEvent`, which happens when any entity falls from a height. It will be used to negate fall damage while a player has a parachute on.

❻ If the entity is not a player, the method returns.

❼ A new variable called `player` is made to store the player that fell.

❽ If the player was not sneaking, then the method returns.

❾ The event is canceled, so the player doesn't take fall damage.

Make sure to import everything. The final code should look like Example 5-5.

Example 5-5. Parachute final code

```
package org.devoxx4kids.forge.mods;

import net.minecraft.entity.player.EntityPlayer;
import net.minecraftforge.event.entity.living.LivingFallEvent;
import net.minecraftforge.fml.common.eventhandler.SubscribeEvent;
import net.minecraftforge.fml.common.gameevent.TickEvent.PlayerTickEvent;

public class Parachute {

        @SubscribeEvent
        public void deployParachute(PlayerTickEvent event){
                EntityPlayer player = event.player;
                if (!player.isAirBorne || !player.isSneaking()) {
                        return;
                }

                event.entity.motionY = -0.05;
        }

        @SubscribeEvent
        public void negateFallDamage(LivingFallEvent event) {
                if (!(event.entity instanceof EntityPlayer)) {
                        return;
                }

        EntityPlayer player = (EntityPlayer) event.entity;

        if (!player.isSneaking()) {
                return;
        }

        event.setCanceled(true);
        }
}
```

Registering this mod is a bit different than the other mods, as the two events here are part of two different buses. `PlayerTickEvent` is part of `FMLCommonHan dler.instance().bus()`, while `LivingFallEvent` is part of `Minecraft Forge.EVENT_BUS`. To register this mod, use the code shown in Example 5-6.

Example 5-6. Registering the parachute mod

```
FMLCommonHandler.instance().bus().register(new Parachute());
MinecraftForge.EVENT_BUS.register(new Parachute());
```

Now you can test out your mod in Minecraft. Log in to your world and jump using the super jump mod. When you are in the air, press Shift to sneak, and your parachute should activate. This is illustrated in Figure 5-3.

Figure 5-3. The parachute in action

Wall-Climbing Golems

Spiders are the only entities in Minecraft that can climb, and they are limited to walls that are three blocks high. This last mod enables snow golems and iron golems to climb walls of any height.

To start, make a new class called `GolemWallClimb` and add an event handler. Register it in the main file and add the code shown here:

```
@SubscribeEvent
public void climbWall(LivingUpdateEvent event) { ❶
        if (!(event.entity instanceof EntitySnowman) &&
                !(event.entity instanceof EntityIronGolem)) { ❷
                return;
        }

        if (!event.entity.isCollidedHorizontally) { ❸
                return;
        }

        event.entity.motionY = 0.5; ❹
}
```

❶ This method runs on a `LivingUpdateEvent`, which happens every tick for every entity.

❷ If the entity is not a snow golem or an iron golem, the method returns.

❸ If the entity is not collided horizontally, the method returns. An entity would be collided horizontally if it is pushing against a block or another entity.

Normally, if an entity is colliding against a block, nothing happens. In this case, the golem's Y motion is set to 0.5, making it move upward. So every time the golem collides, the Y motion is increased by 0.5.

The completed class should now look like Example 5-7.

Example 5-7. Wall-climbing golems final code

```
package org.devoxx4kids.forge.mods;

import net.minecraft.entity.monster.EntityIronGolem;
import net.minecraft.entity.monster.EntitySnowman;
import net.minecraft.entity.player.EntityPlayer;
import net.minecraftforge.event.entity.living.LivingEvent.LivingUpdateEvent;
import net.minecraftforge.fml.common.eventhandler.SubscribeEvent;

public class GolemWallClimb {

        @SubscribeEvent
        public void climbWall(LivingUpdateEvent event) {
                if (!(event.entity instanceof EntitySnowman) &&
                        !(event.entity instanceof EntityIronGolem)) {
                        return;
                }

                if (!event.entity.isCollidedHorizontally) {
                        return;
                }

                event.entity.motionY = 0.5;
        }

}
```

Now, you are ready to try your mod. Import everything and run Minecraft by clicking the green arrow in Eclipse.

Create a golem, make a wall that is wide enough so that the golem doesn't go around it, and push the golem against the wall. Figure 5-4 shows an example of a wall-climbing golem.

Figure 5-4. Wall-climbing iron golem

The golem will climb a wall for only a few blocks if there isn't a mob on the top of it. If you spawn a mob like a zombie or a skeleton on the wall, and the golem notices it, then the golem will try to climb the entire wall to get to the mob.

This mod can be updated to allow any entity to climb up the wall by changing the first if statement in the event handler. Try to make a villager or a cow climb up the wall.

Summary

In this chapter, we created a few mods that involved movement of entities. The first allowed players to jump higher, and the second added a parachute in order to negate fall damage from the higher jump. The final mod changed the movement of golems instead of players, and allowed golems to climb walls. If you want to continue working on movement mods, you could try making entities move faster, making certain blocks stop movement, or increasing entities' swimming speed.

You also learned arithmetic operators for multiplication, and even combined operators so you can multiply and assign using *=. The logical or operator, ||, was also used in one of the mods.

The next chapter will teach you how to create new commands with Forge.

CHAPTER 6

New Commands

In this chapter, you'll learn how to add new commands to the game and customize them to your liking. Minecraft already has many commands—for example, the /summon command lets you spawn an entity wherever you want to, and /setblock lets you place a block anywhere you wish. Each new command you create using Forge requires two things: first, a new file containing the command's details, and second, a line in a new method that registers the command in the main file. This chapter has a lot more Java code than the previous ones, so pay attention carefully.

The first command you will create will spawn a specified number of flaming pigs at the sender's location. This can be used for fun things like a cloud of particles or tons of porkchops. Then, you will make a command that lets you choose two locations, and when you use the command, the area between the two locations gets filled with the block of your choice.

Flaming Pigs

In Minecraft, pigs aren't normally on fire. The only way to ignite them is to push them into a fire block or into lava. This mod will add a command that lets you spawn whatever number of pigs you want and also sets them on fire. It isn't really very useful —it's just funny to see a bunch of pigs on fire. And isn't that what the entire game of Minecraft is about?

First, create a new class and call it FlamingPigs. This will be the file that stores all of the command's details. We will fill in all the details of this class later. Server commands are registered by handling the FMLServerStartingEvent. Open your main file, find the init() method, and add the code from Example 6-1 directly after it.

Example 6-1. Register the flaming pigs command

```
@EventHandler
public void registerCommands(FMLServerStartingEvent event) {
        event.registerServerCommand(new FlamingPigs());
}
```

The method in this code goes underneath the method where FMLInitializationE
vent is handled, specifically after the closing } of the init method. Note the
@EventHandler annotation above the method registers it as an event handler.

You will get an error because the class FlamingPigs does not implement the *interface*
ICommand.

Classes define methods that perform various actions, such as registering a command,
initializing the mod, and so on. The code that gets executed as part of this action is
defined within the method scope and between { and }. The methods together are
called *class behavior*.

An interface is a Java concept that allows you to define common behavior across different classes using methods. Other Java classes can then *implement* a Java interface
and provide the actual code for that method.

For example, you might have an interface called Shape with a method named area,
and two classes, Circle and Square, that want to have the common behavior. This is
done by *implementing* the Shape interface.

For example, consider an interface called Shape that can be used to define any shape,
with a method named area that can be used to find the area of any given shape. It
also has two classes, Circle and Square (representing circle and square shapes,
respectively), that implement the Shape interface. The area of these two shapes is calculated differently, so implementation of the area method would be done accordingly. This is shown in Example 6-2.

Example 6-2. Interface sample code

```
interface Shape {
        public float area();
}

class Circle implements Shape {
        public float area() {
                return Math.PI * radius * radius;
        }
}

class Square implements Shape {
        public float area() {
```

```
        return side * side;
    }
}
```

The area of a circle can be calculated by multiplying the mathematical constant pi by the square of the radius of the circle, whereas the area of a square shape is the length squared. These different implementations are shown in the area() method of the Circle and Square classes in the preceding code block.

In order to make FlamingPigs implement ICommand, you need to add two words—implements ICommand—right after the class name, public class FlamingPigs, but before the bracket on the same line.

Your class should now look like Example 6-3.

Example 6-3. Flaming pigs command class after implementation

```
package org.devoxx4kids.forge.mods;

import net.minecraft.command.ICommand;

public class FlamingPigs implements ICommand {

}
```

You will get an error telling you that you need to add in some methods. This is because whenever you implement a class, you also need to implement its methods or common behavior, as we explained earlier. Add the methods shown in Example 6-4. The complete list of methods is broken into two parts, and the relevant methods are all explained. The methods that are not explained will not be used but are added because they have to be, as they are part of the ICommand interface.

Example 6-4. Flaming pigs method code part 1

```
private List aliases = new ArrayList();  ❶
private int numberOfPigs = 0;  ❷

public FlamingPigs() {  ❸
        aliases.add("flamingpigs");  ❹
        aliases.add("fp");
}

@Override
public int compareTo(Object o) {
        return 0;
}

@Override  ❺
```

```
public String getCommandUsage(ICommandSender sender) { ❻
        return "/flamingpigs <number of pigs>";
}

@Override
public List getAliases() { ❼
        return aliases;
}
```

❶ List is a Java utility class that is a collection of values that can be written to and read from. ArrayList is a type of List where values are arranged in a sequence and can be added or accessed in any order. This line creates a new ArrayList called aliases. This ArrayList stores all of the names that can be typed to run the command.

❷ This line creates a variable that will contain the number of pigs to be spawned when the command is sent.

❸ This line is the *constructor*, which is a special method in the class that runs when the class is initialized. The constructor methods have the same name as the class, and that's what makes them special. In this case, it will run when it is registered in the main file.

❹ This line and the one after it add the string values flamingpigs and fp into the ArrayList aliases.

❺ This @Override annotation tells the class to use this method instead of the default one from the implemented class, ICommand. Any method in this class with this annotation tells the Java compiler that this method is implementing a method from an interface, or *overriding* a method.

❻ This method gets the usage of the command. In this case, the command should be used as /flamingpigs or /fp, and then a number value should be given indicating the number of pigs to be spawned.

ICommandSender is a Forge class that lets the command get more information about the player, send chat messages to the player, and has other methods too.

❼ This method returns a list of all the aliases for the command. Because an Array List is a type of List, the ArrayList aliases works here. Now, instead of only being able to use /flamingpigs as the command, you can also use /fp.

Now, you can add the method code in Example 6-5 directly underneath the code from Example 6-4.

Example 6-5. Flaming pigs method code part 2

```
@Override
public void execute(ICommandSender sender, String[] args) { ❶
        if (args.length != 1) { ❷
                sendErrorMessage(sender, "Invalid number of arguments!"); ❸
                return;
        }

        try { ❹
                numberOfPigs = Integer.parseInt(args[0]);
        } catch(NumberFormatException e) { ❺
                sendErrorMessage(sender, "The argument \"" + args[0] +
                        "\" is not a valid number!");
                return;
        }

        EntityPlayer player = (EntityPlayer) sender; ❻

        for (int i = 0 ; i < numberOfPigs ; i++) { ❼
                EntityPig pig = new EntityPig(player.worldObj); ❽
                pig.setLocationAndAngles(player.posX, player.posY, player.posZ, 0, 0);
                pig.setFire(10000);
                player.worldObj.spawnEntityInWorld(pig);
        }
}

private void sendErrorMessage(ICommandSender sender, String message) { ❾
        sender.addChatMessage(new ChatComponentText(
                EnumChatFormatting.DARK_RED + message));
}

@Override
public boolean canCommandSenderUse(ICommandSender sender) { ❿
        return sender instanceof EntityPlayer;
}

@Override
public List addTabCompletionOptions(ICommandSender sender,
                String[] args, BlockPos pos) {
        return null;
}

@Override
public boolean isUsernameIndex(String[] args, int index) {
        return false;
}
```

❶ This method executes the code when the command is run by a player. The parameters to this method are important. The first parameter, ICommandSender sender, provides the player/command block/console that sent the command. The second parameter, String[] args, is an *array* of string items, and contains a list of all the arguments to the command.

An *array* is a Java concept that allows a fixed number of items of similar types to be stored together in a list. Each item in an array is called an *element*, and each element is indexed by its *numerical index*. The first element is available at index 0, and each nth element is at n–1 index. For example, the sixth element will be at index 5. The total length of an array is available using the *length* property. In our case, the first element of the array is available at args[0], and length can be read using args.length.

An *argument* is anything after the actual command. For example, if a player ran the command /fp 10, then 10 would be the argument.

❷ Our mod requires only a single argument that provides the number of pigs that need to be spawned. The if statement checks whether the length of the args array is not equal to 1.

❸ If the if statement in the previous line is true, the player is sent a dark red chat message telling them that they did not enter the right number of arguments. This is done by calling a newly created sendErrorMessage method on ❾.

❹ This line is the start of a try-catch statement. A try-catch statement in Java is used to find error conditions in the code, or *exceptions*, and deal with them. The code that can possibly throw an error is put inside the try block. The errors that can be thrown are represented by a Java class. Each error is specified on a catch block. The code that needs to get executed when the exception is caught is put inside the catch block.

The try block is trying to turn the first argument, identified by args[0], into an integer, and then set the numberOfPigs variable to the value made. This is accomplished with the method Integer.parseInt().

❺ The catch block is using the Java class java.lang.NumberFormatException to catch the exception, which is thrown when a string cannot be converted into an integer. The argument must be an integer, because we want a number of pigs. In this case, the player who ran the command is notified that the number they put in is invalid.

Notice that there are three quotation marks in each of the string values, but they have a backslash behind them. This is called *escaping*. The backslashes are telling Java that the quotation marks directly ahead are not defining the boundaries of the string. That way, you can put quotation marks in a string value. After sending the message, the method returns.

❻ A variable of the type EntityPlayer is made by casting sender to the Entity Player class.

❼ A for loop is created, and it will run for the number of times specified in number OfPigs.

❽ A new variable is created to store an EntityPig. The pig's location is set to that of the player who sent the command. The pig is set on fire for 10,000 ticks, or 500 seconds. This is good enough time for a pig to die. The pig is then spawned into the world that the player who sent the command is in.

All this code is inside the for loop, so it will run as many times as specified by numberOfPigs.

❾ sendErrorMessage is a new method that sends a chat message to the player in a dark red color.

❿ This method tells Forge whether or not the player/command block/console who sent the command can use it. An if statement is used to check whether the sender is a player. If the sender is indeed a player, then true is returned, indicating that the command can run. If the sender is not a player, the method returns false and the command does not run.

Make sure to import everything. You are now ready to test out your new mod. Launch Minecraft using the green arrow and try out your new command. Make sure you put in a valid number after the command, and that you put only one argument. Start with spawning about 10 pigs by issuing the following command:

```
/flamingpigs 10
```

And now you can see 10 pigs are spawned at your current location and they are all set on fire. Don't spawn too many pigs, or your game will crash. A good limit is about 100.

Figure 6-1 shows what happens when you use the flaming pigs command with a high number.

Figure 6-1. Flaming pigs

A fun way to use this mod is by using the contraption shown in Figure 6-2. Stand on top of the hopper and use the /fp command. When the pigs spawned by the command die, their drops will go into the hopper and ultimately into the chest. This way, if you have the "pigs dropping diamonds" mod installed, you can easily get diamonds.

Figure 6-2. Flaming pigs hopper contraption

Block Filler

Have you ever felt the need to fill an area with a particular block? For example, maybe you've wanted to create a giant mansion or an arena to fight mobs in. This new command allows you to select two positions as corners, and then fill in the space between with any block you want. The positions will be set by right-clicking or left-clicking blocks with a wooden axe. The positions can be selected in one, two, and three dimensions.

This mod will utilize both event handlers and commands.

First, create a new event handler class and call it `BlockFillerPositionSelector`. You will need to add two variables before you add the method code; these go directly under the line `public class BlockFillerPositionSelector {`:

```
static List<Integer> pos1 = new ArrayList();
static List<Integer> pos2 = new ArrayList();
```

Make sure you import `List`, `Integer`, and `ArrayList`.

The variables are both `ArrayLists`, which are lists that you can read from and write to. They will store the x, y, and z coordinates of the first and second position used in the mod. The `<Integer>` part makes sure that the list can store only integers, and the positions will be only integers. The `ArrayLists` are called `pos1` and `pos2`, short for Position 1 and Position 2.

`static` is a Java keyword that allows `pos1` and `pos2` variables to be shareable among different classes. It also means that `pos1` and `pos2` are not variables that belong to a class instance, but instead they are shared among all instances of that class.

Then, add the method code shown in Example 6-6.

Example 6-6. Block filler event handler method code

```
@SubscribeEvent
public void choosePositions(PlayerInteractEvent event) { ❶
    if (event.entityPlayer.getHeldItem() == null || ❷
        event.entityPlayer.getHeldItem().getItem()
            != Items.wooden_axe ||
        !event.entityPlayer.capabilities.isCreativeMode) {
            return;
    }

    if (event.action == Action.RIGHT_CLICK_BLOCK) { ❸
            pos1.clear(); ❹
            pos1.add(event.pos.getX()); ❺
            pos1.add(event.pos.getY());
            pos1.add(event.pos.getZ());
            event.entityPlayer.addChatMessage(new ChatComponentText( ❻
                    EnumChatFormatting.GREEN
                    + "Position 1 set to "
                    + event.pos.getX()
                    + ", " + event.pos.getY()
                    + ", " + event.pos.getZ() + "."));
            event.setCanceled(true); ❼
    } else if (event.action == Action.LEFT_CLICK_BLOCK) { ❽
            pos2.clear(); ❾
            pos2.add(event.pos.getX());
            pos2.add(event.pos.getY());
            pos2.add(event.pos.getZ());
            event.entityPlayer.addChatMessage(new ChatComponentText(
```

```
                    EnumChatFormatting.GREEN
                    + "Position 2 set to "
                    + event.pos.getX()
                    + ", " + event.pos.getY()
                    + ", " + event.pos.getZ() + "."));
              event.setCanceled(true);
          }
      }
  }
```

❶ This method runs on a `PlayerInteractEvent`, which covers many miscellaneous actions. The ones we need to focus on are right-click and left-click, because right-clicking or left-clicking with a wooden axe will be the way to determine the first and second position.

❷ `||` is a logical operator in Java that can be used to combine multiple boolean conditions into one. The first boolean condition is evaluated. If it is true, then the result of the entire condition is derived to be true. If it is false, the next boolean condition is evaluated. If the result of that evaluation is true, then the result of the entire condition is derived to be true, and so on. In short, any boolean condition needs to evaluate to true for the entire condition to be true.

In this case, three boolean conditions are combined. The first condition checks if the player is holding an item in his hand. If the player is not holding an item, then Forge returns `null`. The second condition checks if the player is holding a wooden axe. Checking the item type without knowing if the player is holding an item would throw an error. So the sequence of checks is important. The third condition checks if the player is not in creative mode. If the command worked in survival mode, the game wouldn't be fun because you could get anything you wanted with a wooden axe. All these conditions need to be true before any further code can run in this method.

❸ `event.action` provides different actions by the player. This `if` statement checks if the action of the event was right-clicking a block. The code inside this block is run if the condition is true.

❹ `clear` is a method on `ArrayList` that clears all the values entered in `pos1`. This is required to clear the values from the last run of this command. Now new co-ordinates can be added to it.

❺ The x, y, and z coordinates of the block that is right-clicked are added to `pos1`.

❻ A green chat message is sent to the player confirming the position selected. If the player clicked the block at x position 54, y position 63, and z position 102, the message would say "Position 1 set to 54, 63, 102." in green letters.

❼   This line cancels the event. This is useful if the player needs to select a block with a GUI as a position, because it makes sure that the block's GUI does not open. For example, if a player wanted to select a chest as the first position, then it would be annoying if the GUI is opened instead of being selected.

❽   This line checks for a left-click action. Notice the `else if` instead of the `if`; this statement is still part of the `if` statement checking for right-click. It will run only if the right-click part didn't execute—hence the `else`.

❾   This line and the four lines after it do the same thing as the first part of the statement, but with `pos2` instead of `pos1`.

Make sure to import all the classes that will update your source file accordingly. When importing `Action`, import `net.minecraftforge.event.entity.player.Play erInteractEvent.Action`, not any of the other imports. Also, for the `List` import, use `java.util.List`.

Next, we need a class for the command. Create a new class called `BlockFillCommand`. Remember to add `implements ICommand` after the class name.

Most of the methods from the `ICommand` interface were explained in the previous section and are shown in Example 6-7. They provide the command name and usage, list of aliases, and other functionality to Forge. Remember, this code goes between the two brackets in the class.

Example 6-7. Block filler method code part 1

```
private List aliases = new ArrayList();
private Block block; ❶

public BlockFillCommand() {
        aliases.add("fillblocks");
        aliases.add("fb");
}

@Override
public int compareTo(Object o) {
        return 0;
}

@Override
public String getCommandUsage(ICommandSender sender) {
        return "fillblocks <block ID>";
}

@Override
public List getAliases() {
```

```
        return aliases;
}

@Override
public List addTabCompletionOptions(ICommandSender sender,
                String[] args, BlockPos pos) {
        return null;
}

@Override
public boolean isUsernameIndex(String[] args, int index) {
        return false;
}
```

❶ The variable here, block, will be used to store the block that the selected area will be filled with. This will be used from the execute() method, which will be explained next.

execute() is the method where all the action happens, so let's take a closer look at that. The code you need to add is shown in Example 6-8. It goes directly after the code from Example 6-7.

Example 6-8. Block filler method code part 2

```
@Override
public void execute(ICommandSender sender, String[] args) {
        if (args.length != 1) { ❶
                sendErrorMessage(sender, "Invalid number of arguments!");
                return;
        }

        try { ❷
            block = Block.getBlockById(Integer.parseInt(args[0]));

            if (block == Blocks.air && Integer.parseInt(args[0]) != 0) { ❸
                    sendErrorMessage(sender, "The argument \"" + args[0]
                                    + "\" is not a valid block ID!");
                    return;
            }
        } catch (NumberFormatException e) { ❹
                if (Block.getBlockFromName(args[0]) == null) {
                        sendErrorMessage(sender, "The argument \"" + args[0]
                                        + "\" is not a valid block name!");
                        return;
                } else {
                        block = Block.getBlockFromName(args[0]);
                }
        }

        if (BlockFillerPositionSelector.pos1.isEmpty() ❺
```

```
                || BlockFillerPositionSelector.pos2.isEmpty()) {
            sendErrorMessage(sender, "Make a region selection first!");
            return;
    }

    if (BlockFillerPositionSelector.pos1.get(0) >
            BlockFillerPositionSelector.pos2.get(0)) { ❻
        swapPositions(0);
    }

    if (BlockFillerPositionSelector.pos1.get(1) >
            BlockFillerPositionSelector.pos2.get(1)) {
        swapPositions(1);
    }

    if (BlockFillerPositionSelector.pos1.get(2) >
            BlockFillerPositionSelector.pos2.get(2)) {
        swapPositions(2);
    }

    for (int x = BlockFillerPositionSelector.pos1.get(0);
            x <= BlockFillerPositionSelector.pos2.get(0);
            x++) { ❼
        for (int y = BlockFillerPositionSelector.pos1.get(1);
                y <= BlockFillerPositionSelector.pos2.get(1);
                y++) {
            for (int z = BlockFillerPositionSelector.pos1.get(2);
                z <= BlockFillerPositionSelector.pos2.get(2);
                z++) {
                    ((EntityPlayer) sender)
                        .worldObj
                        .setBlockState(
                            new BlockPos(x, y, z),
                            block.getBlockState().getBaseState()); ❽
            }
        }
    }
}

private void swapPositions(int index){ ❾
        int temp = BlockFillerPositionSelector.pos1.get(index);
        BlockFillerPositionSelector.pos1.set(index,
            BlockFillerPositionSelector.pos2.get(index));
        BlockFillerPositionSelector.pos2.set(index, temp);
}

private void sendErrorMessage(ICommandSender sender, String message) { ❿
        sender.addChatMessage(new ChatComponentText(
            EnumChatFormatting.DARK_RED + message));
}

@Override
```

```
public boolean canCommandSenderUse(ICommandSender sender) {
    return sender instanceof EntityPlayer;
}
```

❶ Command requires only one argument (i.e., the ID of the block that will be used to fill the selected area). If the number of arguments is not 1, the player is notified of this and the method returns.

❷ This is the start of a try-catch statement that will determine the block that will be used to fill the selected area. The code inside the try block will try to set the block variable to the block with the ID given.

❸ Like ||, && is a logical operator in Java that can be used to combine multiple boolean conditions into one. The first boolean condition is evaluated. If it is false, then the entire statement is derived to be false. If it is true, then the next boolean condition is evaluated. If it is false, then the result of the entire condition is derived to be false, and so on. In short, all boolean conditions need to evaluate to true for the entire condition to be true.

In the game, 0 is the ID of air. This if statement checks if the block is air and if the ID of the block is not 0. If this is true, then the ID is invalid, the player is notified by a an error message, and the method returns.

❹ Converting a string to a number can throw an error (e.g., if a letter or a word is entered instead of a number). Java will throw an error that can be caught as Num berFormatException. If one was thrown, then the argument typed in the command was not a number. Then, an if statement checks whether a block can be made from the given name. If not, the method returns after the player is sent a message indicating that the block name is invalid. If the name is valid, the block variable is set to whatever block is made from the block name given.

❺ isEmpty() is a method of ArrayList class that returns true if the list is empty (i.e., contains no elements). This happens for us when the player gives the command without doing both left-click and right-click. The if statement checks whether two positions are selected. If one or both of them are empty, the player is notified of this and the method returns.

❻ The blocks are placed from lower x, y, and z value to the higher. This if statement and the next two if statements after it make pos1 have the lower of all three values. To do this, the if statements use the greater-than operator (>). If pos1 is greater than pos2, then they are swapped using the swapPositions method. The blocks are then placed by a for loop that starts with the coordinate from pos1 and goes up to the coordinate from pos2, so pos1 has to have the lower value of the two.

❼ These are three nested for loops. Placing one loop inside the body of another loop is called *nesting*. For nested loops, the outer loop defines the number of complete repetitions of the inner loop. The loops can be nested to any level.

In our case, the outermost loop is for the x-axis, the second for the y-axis, and the third for the z-axis. The for loops start at the value from pos1, and then increment by one until the first value is greater than (not <=, or less than or equal to) the value from pos2.

The blocks are laid on the z-axis first, then on the y-axis, and finally on the x-axis. In other words, the for loop goes forward by one x coordinate, and then goes up on the y-axis until it reaches the second y coordinate. Each time the loop goes up the y-axis, the loop inside the y for loop places blocks on the z-axis.

❽ A block is placed at the x, y, and z variables in the for loops, and the block's type is determined by the block variable.

❾ A new method is added to our class that allows us to swap the positions of two values. This is easily done by storing the original value in a temporary variable, copying the new value in place of the original value, and then storing the value from the temporary variable in place of the new value. This method is called thrice while determining the lower of the pos1 and pos2 values, once each for x, y, and z coordinates.

❿ If an error occurs (for example, if the command receives a letter as input instead of a number), then display a message to the user in a dark red color.

To register the command, put the text event.registerServerCommand(new Block FillCommand()); in your registerCommands method in your main file. Make sure you do this, because the command will not work otherwise.

Make sure to import everything. You are now ready to try out your mod in Minecraft. As always, click the green arrow on the top to run the game.

In order to test this mod, get a wooden axe from your inventory, click on two places far apart, and issue the following command:

```
/fillblocks 46
```

This will fill up the selected area between the two clicks with TNT. Why TNT? 46 is the block ID of TNT. If you want to do it for a different block from vanilla Minecraft, then you already know how to find the ID for it.

The two selected corners are opposite corners of a rectangular prism. Feel free to be creative and make some fun structures.

One fun example of a way you can use this mod is making a huge TNT bomb. An image of this is shown in Figure 6-3.

Figure 6-3. Block filled with a huge TNT bomb

The crater made by lighting the bomb is shown in Figure 6-4.

Figure 6-4. Aftermath of the TNT bomb created using the block filler

You can also use this mod to build cool structures like arenas or mansions.

Summary

In this chapter, you learned how to make new commands with Forge. You added a simple command that spawned any number of flaming pigs at your location. Then, you made a more complex command that let you fill areas with blocks. You are encouraged to create more commands and customize the experience of your game. For example, with the knowledge you now have, you can spawn a creeper at your current location. The GitHub repo of this book also has some additional commands for you to try.

In the process of learning these new commands, some Java concepts such as arrays and the `ArrayList` class were introduced. We also explained basic error handling using `try-catch`, escaping special characters (such as quotes) within a string, and the logical `&&` operator.

The next chapter will teach you how to do what many modders want to do: add a new block.

CHAPTER 7

New Block

Have you ever wanted to add a new block to the game? Most modders want to. Whether it's because the regular blocks are too mundane, or you have a great idea for a new block, making a new block is fun, and there are a lot of features that you can customize. This chapter will explain how to create a new block and will have an ender theme. However, you can make tons of other kinds of blocks, such as stairs or teleporters, and variations like those will be explained here.

The new block that we will create will be called an *Enderium Block*, but you can change the name if you change the block. For example, if you change the block to be glass stairs, you would rename the block *Glass Stairs*.

This mod will be a bit different from all the other ones so far, because it does not use event handlers. Instead, it uses a new class to store all of the block's details, and then registers it to the *game registry*. Making a new block also allows for a lot of customization, so a few variations of the block will be shown as well.

Creating the Block Class

The first thing you will need is a new class that stores all of the block's information, like the hardness, resistance, and creative tab. Make a new class called `EnderBlock` in your package. The first thing you need to do is make the class extend from `Block`. This means `EnderBlock` becomes a child class, and `Block` is the parent class. `Block` is a Java class in Minecraft that enables any Java class to look and act like a block.

Replace all of the generated code with the code from Example 7-1. This can be done by deleting all of the current code, and then copying and pasting this code into your file.

Example 7-1. New block finished class

```java
package org.devoxx4kids.forge.mods;

import net.minecraft.block.Block;
import net.minecraft.block.material.Material;
import net.minecraft.creativetab.CreativeTabs;

public class EnderBlock extends Block {

        public EnderBlock() {  ❶
                super(Material.iron);  ❷
                this.setUnlocalizedName("enderBlock");  ❸
                this.setCreativeTab(CreativeTabs.tabBlock);  ❹
                this.setResistance(5.0F);  ❺
                this.setHardness(10.0F);  ❻
                this.setLightLevel(1.0F);  ❼
        }
}
```

❶ This is the start of the constructor. The `public` modifier allows this constructor to be accessed by other classes.

❷ `super` is a special Java method and calls the *super constructor*, which is a constructor of the parent class.

   If multiple classes are inherited from a parent class and they all need to set some property value, then it makes more sense to set that property in the parent class and pass the actual value from the child class. That's what is being done here.

   The super constructor in this case requires a parameter for the material of the block, and in this case it is set to `Material.iron`.

❸ A block/item has two names: the *unlocalized name* and the *localized name*. The unlocalized name is what is used in the code that we write, and the localized name is the one that is shown in the game. These names are mapped to each other in a *.lang* file, which you will learn about later.

   This line sets the block's unlocalized name to `enderBlock` by using the `setUnloca lizedName()` method. `this` is a Java keyword and refers to the current Java object. The unlocalized name can be anything you want, as long as it is not the same as another block/item's unlocalized name. This means that the unlocalized name must be unique in a *.lang* file.

❹ This line adds the block to the Blocks creative tab. Without adding the block to a creative tab, the only way to get the block would be to give it to yourself with the `/give` command, which is a standard Minecraft command.

tabBlock is the most logical place to add this block. However, you can also add this block to a different tab. You can see a complete list of tabs where this block can be added by placing the cursor right after CreativeTabs. and pressing the Ctrl-Enter keys. The tabBlock can be replaced with any of the values shown in this list. So if this block was to be shown in the Miscellaneous tab, then tabBlock would need to be replaced with tabMisc.

❺ This line sets the block's resistance to 5.0F. The resistance of a block is its resistance to explosions. For example, obsidian has a resistance of 2000.0F, so it cannot be destroyed by explosions. Diamond ore has a resistance of 5.0F, and iron block has a resistance of 10.0F. This block has a low resistance, so it can be easily destroyed by an explosion.

Feel free to change this value to any number, but don't go below 0.0. Lower resistance means that its easier to destroy a block by an explosion. Higher resistance means its harder to destroy it by an explosion.

❻ The hardness of a block dictates how fast the block will be broken. The higher the hardness, the slower the block is broken. This line sets the hardness of this block to 10.0F. For example, end stone block has a hardness of 3.0F, and glass has a hardness of 0.3F.

❼ This sets the block's light level to 1.0 so that it will glow brightly and look awesome.

Now your block class is ready, but we still need to register the block in the main file.

Registering Your Block

Now, you need to register your block in the main file. First, create a variable in the main file as shown here (this variable will store the block in the form of the class you just made, and it goes directly after the first bracket):

```
public static Block enderBlock;
```

 Java naming conventions use *camelcasing*. Camelcasing is where you make the first letter of the first word lowercase, and the first letter of all of the other words uppercase. For example, EnderBlock in camelcasing would be enderBlock. Camelcasing is the preferred way of naming variables, but it is not the only way. For example, in this code, the words are separated with underscores.

Now, add the code shown here to your init() method in your main file:

```
enderBlock = new EnderBlock();  ❶
GameRegistry.registerBlock(enderBlock, "enderBlock");  ❷
```

❶ Initializes `enderBlock` variable of the type `EnderBlock()`.

❷ `GameRegistry` is a Forge class and is a central store where new items, blocks, recipes, aliases, and the like can be registered and searched.

In this case, `enderBlock` is registered in the `GameRegistry`, with the name `ender Block`. Note that the name here is neither the localized or the unlocalized name. This is a mod-unique name to register it as is, and will get prefixed by your `modid`.

Now that you have registered your block, the only thing remaining is to give it a localized name.

Naming Your Block

For this part, you will need to create a new file in a specific directory. Navigate to your Forge folder where you ran the `gradlew` command in Chapter 1. If you followed the instructions as is, then this would be the *forge/* directory on your Desktop. If you used a different name or location, navigate to the directory that you created instead.

Inside that folder, there should be another folder called *src/*. Navigate to that folder, then to *main/*, then to *resources/*. This should look like the screenshot shown in Figure 7-1.

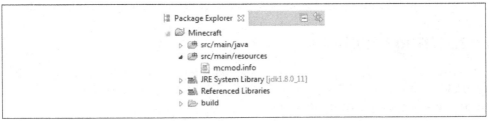

Figure 7-1. src/main/resources folder

Right-click that folder, navigate to New→Folder, and create another folder called *assets*. Right-click again on that folder and create a new folder. Give it the same name as the value of mod's `MODID` field. The name can technically be anything, but it is best to give it the name of your `MODID` because that is the folder you will be using for textures later. The `MODID` that was suggested in the beginning of this book was `myMods`. If you used that `MODID`, then your folder should be called *mymods*, which is `myMods` in lowercase letters, because Forge always looks for a folder with lowercase letters. In the folder you just created, make another folder called *lang*. The updated folder will look like the screenshot shown in Figure 7-2.

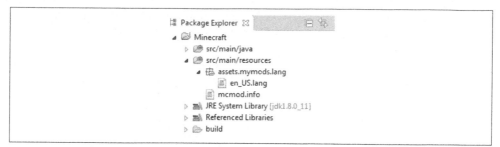

Figure 7-2. src/main/resources/assets/mymods/lang folder

At first, you will see three different folders: *assets*, *assets.mymods*, and *assets.mymods.lang*. Don't worry, these will merge by themselves later.

This folder stores a bunch of *.lang* files that give translations of block names in different languages. In this one, we will be using only English. Right-click your *lang* folder, and navigate to New→File. Name the file *en_US.lang* and open it up. Add the text `tile.enderBlock.name=Enderium Block`.

Do not change anything here except for the name after the = if you want to. Do not put spaces directly before or after the = either, or it will not work. Notice that the first part is `tile.enderBlock.name` instead of just `enderBlock`. The `tile.` and `.name` parts are automatically added by Minecraft. This is the complete unlocalized name of your block. The text after = is the localized name.

Save the file before you continue.

The `en` in this name refers to the English language, and `US` refers to the United States. If you live in Canada, then you'll create a file called *en_CA.lang* instead. Similarly, *fr_FR.lang* should be used for French readers living in France, and *fr_BE.lang* should be used for French readers in Belgium. The exact filename is decided by the language and the country you are living in and is defined in "JDK 8 and JRE 8 Supported Locales" (*http://bit.ly/1bt4idl*).

This mapping of the unlocalized name to the localized name is an important programming fundamental called *localization*. This allows a standard name to be used in the code and the actual translation to be defined in the appropriate *.lang* file.

Running Minecraft and Verifying the Mod

Your block is now ready to go!

Start up your game by clicking the green arrow and go to the Building Blocks tab. Scroll all the way down, and you should see a block that looks like a purple-and-black checkerboard, as shown in Figure 7-3. It may be in a different place than the picture because Forge automatically assigns IDs to blocks and items, and the IDs can vary. The blocks in creative tabs are listed by ID, so the block's place could change.

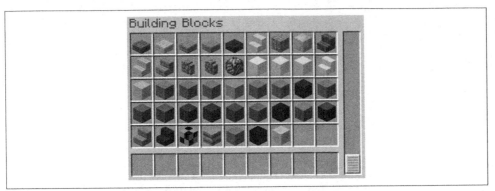

Figure 7-3. New block in the creative tab

When you place it, it should look like Figure 7-4.

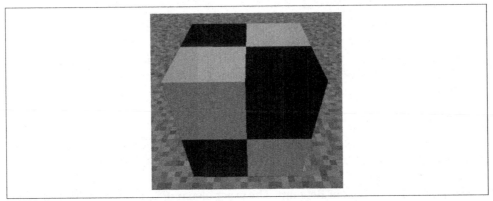

Figure 7-4. New block without a texture

This block is using the default purple-and-black texture, but we'll fix that in Chapter 9.

So you created your very own block. Doesn't that make you feel excited?

This block is like any other regular block except that you have more control over how it behaves. If you've already read Chapter 6, then you know how to write new commands. In that case, you may consider using this block with the /fillblocks command. You'll need to know the block ID, which can be identified in Minecraft via the usual means. On Windows, the display of block IDs can be toggled by pressing the F3 and H keys together. On Mac, this can be achieved by pressing the Fn, F3, and H keys together.

Variations of the New Block

Now that you have a regular block working, you can customize it! This section will show you a bunch of different ways to make your block more interesting.

Block Changer

Sometimes, when you are playing in survival mode, you just don't have enough materials. This variation will aim to change that. Whenever you place an Enderium Block on another block, the Enderium Block will turn into the block underneath it.

To make this change, you will need to add a new method in the EnderBlock class, as shown in Example 7-2.

Example 7-2. Block changer method code

```
@Override ❶
public void onBlockAdded(World world, BlockPos pos, IBlockState state) { ❷
        IBlockState block = world.getBlockState(pos.add(0, -1, 0)); ❸
        world.setBlockState(pos, block); ❹
        EntityLightningBolt lightning = new EntityLightningBolt(world, ❺
                                    pos.getX(), pos.getY(), pos.getZ());
        world.addWeatherEffect(lightning); ❻
}
```

❶ This annotation shows that this class is overriding the method from the parent Block class.

❷ The onBlockAdded() method runs whenever the block is placed, and it has three parameters you can use: the world the block is in defined by world, the position of the block defined by pos, and the state of the block defined by state.

❸ This line gets the state of the block underneath the Enderium Block and saves it to a variable called block.

❹ The Enderium Block is set to the block underneath it by using the block variable.

❺ This line makes a new lightning bolt entity at the position of the block.

❻ The lightning bolt is spawned into the world, just for special effects.

Once you import everything, you are ready to test out your mod. Run Minecraft by clicking the green arrow on the top, log in to your game, and put an Enderium Block in your inventory. Place it down on whatever block you want, and it should turn into that block.

Majestic Enderium Block

Some blocks, like chests and furnaces, do something when you right-click them. Some open up a GUI, some explode, and some make a redstone signal. This variation of the ender block will make it spawn an ender eye entity when you right-click it. It will also send you a chat message saying that you have clicked the block.

In the EnderBlock class, add the method shown in Example 7-3.

Example 7-3. The Majestic Enderium Block method code

```
@Override ❶
public boolean onBlockActivated(World world,
        int x,
        int y,
        int z,
        EntityPlayer player,
        int i1,
        float f1,
        float f2,
        float f3) {
        if (!world.isRemote) ❷
                return false;

        player.addChatMessage(new ChatComponentText( ❸
                EnumChatFormatting.DARK_PURPLE +
                        "You have clicked on the majestic ENDERIUM BLOCK!!!!!"));
        EntityEnderEye eye = new EntityEnderEye(world,
                x + 0.5,
                y + 1.5,
                z + 0.5); ❹
        eye.motionY = 0.1; ❺
        world.spawnEntityInWorld(eye); ❻
        return true; ❼
}
```

❶ This method is defined in the superclass of this class, Block. The @Override annotation on the method confirms that.

It is called when the block is right-clicked. The return type is boolean, so it has to return true or false. There are nine parameters, but we will be using only the first five. The first one is the world in which the block resides, the next three are the block's coordinates, and the last one is the player who clicked on the block.

❷ If the world is not remote (i.e., this method is called in a server world), then the method returns false. This indicates that nothing else needs to happen in this method.

❸ The rest of the method executes if this method is called in a client world. The player is sent a message indicating that "You have clicked on the majestic ENDERIUM BLOCK!!!!!" in dark purple letters.

❹ `EntityEnderEye` is a Java class in Minecraft that allows you to create an ender eye. A new variable called `eye` of the type `EntityEnderEye` is created, one block above the Enderium Block, and centered.

❺ The ender eye's Y motion is set to 0.1 so it will slowly rise.

❻ The ender eye is spawned into the world.

❼ Finally, the method returns `true`, indicating everything is now completed.

Your `EnderBlock` class should now look like Example 7-4.

Example 7-4. The Majestic Enderium Block final code

```
package org.devoxx4kids.forge.mods;

import net.minecraft.block.Block;
import net.minecraft.block.material.Material;
import net.minecraft.entity.item.EntityEnderEye;
import net.minecraft.entity.player.EntityPlayer;
import net.minecraft.util.ChatComponentText;
import net.minecraft.util.EnumChatFormatting;
import net.minecraft.world.World;

public class EnderBlock extends Block {

        public EnderBlock() {
                super(Material.iron);
                this.setUnlocalizedName("enderBlock");
                this.setCreativeTab(CreativeTabs.tabBlock);
                this.setResistance(5.0F);
                this.setHardness(10.0F);
                this.setLightLevel(1.0F);
        }

        public boolean onBlockActivated(World world,
                int x,
                int y,
                int z,
                EntityPlayer player,
                int i1,
                float f1,
                float f2,
                float f3) {
                if (!world.isRemote)
```

```
            return false;

        player.addChatMessage(new ChatComponentText(
                EnumChatFormatting.DARK_PURPLE +
                    "You have clicked on the majestic " +
                    "ENDERIUM BLOCK!!!!!"));
        EntityEnderEye eye = new EntityEnderEye(world,
                x + 0.5,
                y + 1.5,
                z + 0.5);
        eye.motionY = 0.1;
        world.spawnEntityInWorld(eye);
        return true;
    }

}
```

Now you are ready to try out this mod in Minecraft.

As always, run Minecraft by clicking the green arrow. Place an Enderium Block and right-click it. Figure 7-5 shows what happens.

Figure 7-5. The Majestic Enderium Block

Summary

In this chapter, you learned how to make a new block and change its hardness and resistance. It was called an Enderium Block and was a simple, solid block. Then, you saw two variations of it—the first allowed you to change the block that it is placed on, and the second spawned an ender eye entity when you right-clicked the block.

Now that you know how to make a regular block, you can make tons of different types of blocks. For example, you can make it provide a redstone signal, make it an ore that spawns in the world, or make it do something when you stand on it. These examples will not be explained here, but you can search the Internet for tutorials if you want to learn more.

You also learned Java concepts such as *super constructor* and how to localize your Minecraft game to different languages.

In the next chapter, you will make an item to go with the block you just made.

CHAPTER 8

New Item

Now that you have made a new block, it is time to move on to a new item.

Items can do many things. Most items are used for crafting, smelting, and brewing. Some items light fire (e.g., flint and steel, or fire charges), while others can be eaten (e.g., cookies and potatoes). Some items, such as bows or snowballs, do something when you right-click with them. A lot of items don't do much, such as magma cream or iron ingots.

The item created in this chapter will be an ingot. At first, the item will not do anything, but the later parts of the chapter will offer some variations of this item. The first one will make it spawn an enderman on right-click. The second one will make it a food item. The last one will make it drop when you break an Enderium Block.

Creating the Item Class

A new item does not require as much code as a new block, but there are more ways to customize it. First of all, you will need a new class for the item, just as with the block. Call it EnderIngot.

Just as with the new block, replace the generated code with the code in Example 8-1.

Example 8-1. New item final code

```
package org.devoxx4kids.forge.mods;

import net.minecraft.creativetab.CreativeTabs;
import net.minecraft.item.Item;

public class EnderIngot extends Item {

    public EnderIngot() {
```

```
        super();  ❶
        this.setUnlocalizedName("ingotEnder");  ❷
        this.setCreativeTab(CreativeTabs.tabMaterials);  ❸
    }

}
```

❶   Just like the block, this constructor initializes the super constructor. However, this time, the super constructor does not need any parameters.

❷   The unlocalized name is set to ingotEnder.

❸   The item is added to the Materials creative tab.

Now, to finish creating the item, all you need to do is register the item in the main file. First, as with the block, you need to create a variable to store the item. To do so, use the following code:

```
public static Item enderIngot;
```

The variable is the same as the block one, except that it is of the type Item instead of Block and its name is enderIngot.

Now, go into your main file, and add the code shown here into the init() method:

```
enderIngot = new EnderIngot();
GameRegistry.registerItem(enderIngot, "Ender Ingot");
```

Now you are done registering your item.

To add a name to your item, open up your *en_US.lang* file. Add the text shown here:

```
item.ingotEnder.name=Ender Ingot
```

This file creates a mapping of unlocalized name to localized name. This was explained in "Naming Your Block" on page 88.

Notice that instead of tile.ingotEnder.name, it is item.ingotEnder.name, because a tile is a block and an item is an item.

Your item is now finished.

If you launch Minecraft from Eclipse and you put this item in your inventory, it should look like Figure 8-1. You can find the item in the Materials tab, or you can use the Search tab to find it.

Notice that it has the same purple-and-black texture. This is the placeholder for a texture if a valid one cannot be found. This placeholder texture is used because Forge cannot find a valid texture at the location you told it to look in. We will fix this in Chapter 9.

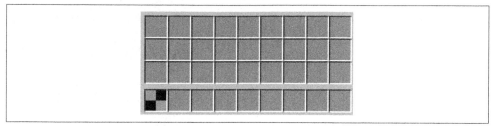

Figure 8-1. New item in the inventory

Variations of the New Item

Now that you have finished the regular item, you can start modifying it to make it more interesting. This section will provide you with some variations of the item that can be made.

Enderman Spawner

The first variation of this item will spawn an enderman whenever you right-click with it. Just like the block, it will use a method from the Item class to do so.

In your item class, add the code shown here under the code for the constructor, but before the last bracket:

```
public ItemStack onItemRightClick(ItemStack stack,
    World world,
    EntityPlayer player) { ❶

    EntityEnderman enderman = new EntityEnderman(world); ❷
    enderman.setLocationAndAngles(player.posX, player.posY, player.posZ, 0, 0); ❸

    world.spawnEntityInWorld(enderman); ❹

    if (!player.capabilities.isCreativeMode) { ❺
        stack.stackSize--;
    }

    return stack; ❻
}
```

❶ This method runs when an item is right-clicked with. It has parameters containing the stack of items defined by ItemStack class, the world in which the item was used defined by World class, and the player who used the item defined by EntityPlayer class.

❷ A variable is created to store an enderman in the world that the item was used in.

❸ The enderman is moved to the player's coordinates by calling the `setLocationAn
dAngles` method on the newly created variable.

❹ The enderman is spawned into the world.

❺ If the player is not in creative mode, the `ItemStack` in that player's hand loses one
item. This allows our item to behave like all other items.

❻ The `ItemStack` is returned, and the method sets the player's held item to the
stack returned.

The class should now look like Example 8-2.

Example 8-2. Enderman spawner final code

```
package org.devoxx4kids.forge.mods;

import net.minecraft.creativetab.CreativeTabs;
import net.minecraft.entity.monster.EntityEnderman;
import net.minecraft.entity.player.EntityPlayer;
import net.minecraft.item.Item;
import net.minecraft.item.ItemStack;
import net.minecraft.world.World;

public class EnderIngot extends Item {

    public EnderIngot() {
        super();
        this.setUnlocalizedName("ingotEnder");
        this.setCreativeTab(CreativeTabs.tabMaterials);
    }

    public ItemStack onItemRightClick(ItemStack stack,
        World world,
        EntityPlayer player) {

        EntityEnderman enderman = new EntityEnderman(world);
        enderman.setLocationAndAngles(player.posX, player.posY, player.posZ,
                                      0, 0);

        world.spawnEntityInWorld(enderman);

        if (!player.capabilities.isCreativeMode) {
            stack.stackSize--;
        }

        return stack;
    }
```

}

Now, you can test out this variation in Minecraft. Log in to your world and right-click with an Ender Ingot. An enderman should spawn at your location. If it spawns but goes away right after, make sure your game difficulty is not set to *peaceful*.

Edible Ingots

This next modification will make the item edible. Food items have a lot of customization options such as potion effects and wolf feeding.

To begin, change the extends statement in EnderIngot class from Item to ItemFood. ItemFood is the superclass for all of the food items in the game. Here's the updated code:

```
extends ItemFood
```

You will get an error because ItemFood has constructors that can only take two or three parameters. This mod will use the three-parameters constructor. The first parameter is the number of hunger bars (1 = 🍖) healed. The second one is how much saturation the food gives you. If your saturation is over 0, you do not get hungry. If your saturation is 0, you can lose hunger. The last parameter, a boolean, determines whether a wolf can eat this food item. The constructor that will be used here is shown next. Replace the old constructor with the new one:

```
super(5, 1.0F, false);
```

This food item gives you 5 hunger points (🍖 🍖 🍖) when you eat it. It gives you a low saturation level because if you actually ate metal, it would probably not be very filling. It also cannot be used as wolf food because there are no wolves we know of that eat metal.

Next, you can add some customization by adding the lines shown here. You don't need to add these, but if you do, they go in the constructor. Don't put them before the super constructor, because the super constructor needs to be first:

```
this.setPotionEffect(1, 60, 2, 0.5F); ❶
this.setAlwaysEdible(); ❷
```

❶ The food is given a potion effect. The method in this line has four parameters.

The first one is the potion ID; in this case, it is 1, which is the ID for speed. The official Minecraft wiki includes a full list of potion IDs (*http://bit.ly/1xysepT*).

The second parameter is the duration of the effect in seconds. This effect will last for a minute.

The third effect is the amplifier. The actual amplifier in the game is always one more than the one in the code. For example, in this mod, the amplifier in the code is 2, so in the game, the effect will be Speed III.

The last parameter is the chance of getting the effect. The chance is out of 1.0F, and so 0.5F means this potion effect will be given to you half the time.

 The food is set so that it can always be eaten, because a player might want to eat it just for saturation or for the speed effect.

You can customize these two parts and the super constructor as much as you like, which is the nice thing about making a food item.

Your class should now look like Example 8-3.

Example 8-3. Edible ingots final code

```
package org.devoxx4kids.forge.mods;

import net.minecraft.item.ItemFood;
import net.minecraft.creativetab.CreativeTabs;

public class EnderIngot extends ItemFood {

        public EnderIngot() {
                super(5, 1.0F, true);
                this.setPotionEffect(1, 60, 2, 0.5F);
                this.setAlwaysEdible();
                this.setUnlocalizedName("ingotEnder");
                this.setCreativeTab(CreativeTabs.tabMaterials);
        }
}
```

After importing everything, you can try out your mod in Minecraft. A picture of a player eating an Ender Ingot is shown in Figure 8-2.

You might not get an effect the first time you eat it, so eat another one if you don't.

Figure 8-2. A player eating an Ender Ingot

Item from Block

This last modification will make Enderium Blocks drop Ender Ingots when they are broken. Note that you must have completed Chapter 7 in order for the code in this section to work properly.

You won't need to change anything in your item class, only in your block class. In your block class, add the two methods shown here:

```
public Item getItemDropped(int i1, Random random, int i2) ❶
{
    return Main.enderIngot; ❷
}

public int quantityDropped(Random random) ❸
{
    return random.nextInt(2) + 3; ❹
}
```

❶ This method gets the item that will be dropped. The parameters of this method are not relevant in this case and so can be ignored.

❷ The method returns `Main.enderIngot`, which is the item you just created. It is using the variable `enderIngot` from the main file as the item.

❸ This method returns the number of items to be dropped.

❹ The method returns a random value between 0 and 2, plus 3. Because 3 is added to the value, the value will range from 3 to 5. The value is recalculated every time.

Your final class should now look like Example 8-4.

Example 8-4. Item from block final code

```
package org.devoxx4kids.forge.mods;

import java.util.Random;

import net.minecraft.block.Block;
import net.minecraft.block.material.Material;
import net.minecraft.entity.item.EntityEnderEye;
import net.minecraft.entity.player.EntityPlayer;
import net.minecraft.item.Item;
import net.minecraft.util.ChatComponentText;
import net.minecraft.util.EnumChatFormatting;
import net.minecraft.world.World;

public class EnderBlock extends Block {

    public EnderBlock() {
        super(Material.iron);
        this.setBlockName("enderBlock");
        this.setCreativeTab(EnderStuff.ender_tab);
        this.setResistance(5.0F);
        this.setHardness(10.0F);
        this.setLightLevel(1.0F);
    }

    public Item getItemDropped(int i1, Random random, int i2)
    {
        return Main.enderIngot;
    }

    public int quantityDropped(Random random)
    {
        return random.nextInt(2) + 3;
    }
}
```

You are now ready to try out your mod in Minecraft. Launch the game, place some Enderium Blocks, switch to survival mode, and break them with a pickaxe. You should receive Ender Ingots.

Summary

In this chapter, you made an item to go along with your block from Chapter 7. Then you learned about some variations of the item such as making it spawn an enderman, making it edible, and making Enderium Blocks drop the item. If you want to experiment more with your new item, try making it launch an arrow when you right-click with it, or teleport you to the End. In the next chapter, you will learn how to make new crafting and smelting recipes, along with textures, to finish off your mod.

CHAPTER 9

Recipes and Textures

Minecraft has three types of recipes: crafting, smelting, and brewing. Each recipe takes an input item and/or block and produces a new item or block. This chapter will teach you how to make new recipes for existing items and blocks in Minecraft and the new ones created earlier in this book. You will learn how to create different types of recipes. You will also learn about ways to customize your recipes by changing the placement, the experience, the items, and other factors.

If you recall, the new blocks that you created in Chapter 7 and the new items that you created in Chapter 8 had a somewhat unappealing purple-and-black texture. This chapter will also teach you how to make textures for them. You will learn about the directory structure of Forge textures and how you can make cool-looking textures for your mod.

Recipes

Forge provides support for all three types of recipes. A crafting recipe can be one of two types: *shaped* or *shapeless*. Smelting and brewing recipes have only one type.

Crafting recipes require items and blocks to be placed on a 2 × 2 or 3 × 3 crafting grid and in turn produce new items and blocks.

A shaped crafting recipe is a recipe that includes items in a certain pattern. For example, a piston has a shaped recipe. It has wood planks in the top row, an iron ingot in the middle, a redstone dust underneath, and cobblestone in the rest of the spaces. The recipe will not work unless you put these items in this exact order.

A shapeless crafting recipe is a bunch of items in the crafting table, in no specific order. For example, the pumpkin pie recipe uses a pumpkin, sugar, and an egg, but these items don't have to be in a specific order for the recipe to work. That means you can place them anywhere in the crafting table as long as you have one of each item.

A smelting recipe is made in a furnace. A furnace takes one item/block and turns it into a different item/block, at the cost of an item to use for fuel. For example, iron ingots are made by smelting iron ore in a furnace.

Brewing recipes create potions by adding various ingredients to water bottles or other potions in a brewing stand. For example, adding blaze powder to an awkward potion will give a potion of strength.

Shaped Crafting Recipe

A crafting table can be a 2 × 2 or 3 × 3 grid, depending on how it's opened. All of the recipes require only one line, but this one is the most complicated.

Let's create a simple recipe that can be created in a 2 × 2 crafting table. For this, we'll craft four dirt blocks into a cobblestone. In the game, it will look like Figure 9-1.

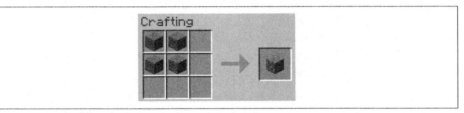

Figure 9-1. Sample 2 × 2 crafting recipe picture

The dirt can be put anywhere in the crafting table as long as it's 2 × 2, as shown in Figure 9-2.

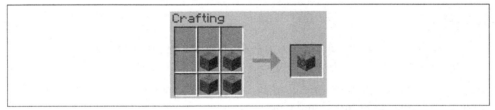

Figure 9-2. Another 2 × 2 crafting recipe picture

The code for this recipe is shown in Example 9-1 and should be added in the `init()` method of your main file.

Example 9-1. 2 × 2 crafting recipe code

```
GameRegistry.addRecipe( ❶
        new ItemStack(Blocks.cobblestone), ❷
        "dd", ❸
        "dd",
        'd', Blocks.dirt); ❹
```

❶ The addRecipe() method of GameRegistry is used to add a shaped recipe.

❷ The result of this recipe will be a stack of items identified by the ItemStack class and contains a cobblestone block.

❸ This is where the recipe is defined. It contains one to three string values in double quotes, separated by commas. Each value defines the position of items and blocks in one or more row(s).

If there is only one value specified, then that defines the placement of items and blocks in any one row of the crafting table. In this case, the placement of items and blocks in other rows does not matter.

If there are two values specified, then that defines the placement of items and blocks in any two consecutive rows of the crafting table. These could be either the top two or bottom two rows, and the placement of items and blocks in other rows does not matter.

If there are three values, then the first value is the first row of the crafting table, the second value is the second row, and the third value is the third row.

Items in each row can be placed in three columns, and each column is represented as a letter. So each row can have up to three letters. If one letter is specified, then that could be any column within that row. If two letters are specified, then that defines the placement of items and blocks in any two consecutive columns of the crafting table for that row. In other words, items and blocks can be placed in two leftmost or two rightmost columns. If three letters are specified, then the first value is the first column, the second value is the second column, and the third value is the third column.

In this case, there are two rows with two ds in each. As only two rows are defined, they can be placed in any two rows of the crafting table. Two ds indicate only two columns. So this will be a 2 × 2 crafting recipe.

The letter d will be assigned to an item/block in the next part of the line.

This line says that the letter d will represent a Dirt block. Notice that the d is in single quotes; this means that the d is going to tell what item/block a letter represents.

This recipe is using d as the letter, but you are free to choose any letter as long the representation of the letter is defined within single quotes as well.

Run Minecraft by clicking the green button in Eclipse. Place a crafting table and try out this recipe. Once you see Cobblestone, try different 2 × 2 positions in the crafting table and you should see the same result.

Now, let's expand this recipe to 3 × 3. We will create a recipe using the items we created in Chapter 8, with the result being the new block from Chapter 7. This recipe will look like Figure 9-3.

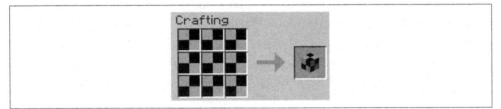

Figure 9-3. Enderium Block crafting recipe

To add the recipe, add the line shown in Example 9-2 in the `init()` method in your main file.

Example 9-2. Shaped recipe for Enderium Blocks

```
GameRegistry.addRecipe( ❶
        new ItemStack(enderBlock), ❷
        "iii", ❸
        "iii",
        "iii",
        'i', enderIngot); ❹
```

❶ The `addRecipe()` method of `GameRegistry` is used to add a shaped recipe.

❷ The result of this recipe will be a stack of items identified by the `ItemStack` class and contains one of the new blocks you made. The new block you made is referred to by its variable `enderBlock`, and the new item you made is referred to as `enderIngot`.

❸ There are three string values in double quotes, and so all three rows will be used in this recipe. Each string value has three characters, and so all three columns will be used in all the rows. That makes it a 3 × 3 recipe.

All of the rows are using i, which will represent an Ender Ingot. So this recipe will require an Ender Ingot in all three rows and all three columns.

❹ This line assigns the letter i to Ender Ingots.

An important thing to remember here is that double quotes indicate rows of a crafting table and single quotes indicate item/block identification. Also, you should never put more than three characters in a double-quote value here.

What if you want to make a recipe where you need multiple item(s)/block(s) as input? What if it's not required to place items in all the rows and/or columns? For that, we will show another recipe for Enderium Blocks, but this one will have empty spaces in it. This is illustrated in Figure 9-4.

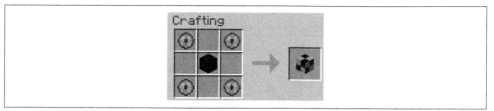

Figure 9-4. Another Enderium Block crafting recipe

Note that four slots are empty here.

The code for this recipe is shown in Example 9-3, and like the other recipes, should go in the init() method of your main file.

Example 9-3. Another shaped recipe for Enderium Blocks

```
GameRegistry.addRecipe( ❶
        new ItemStack(enderBlock), ❷
        "e e", ❸
        " o ",
        "e e",
        'o', Blocks.obsidian,
        'e', Items.ender_eye); ❹
```

❶ The addRecipe method of GameRegistry is used to add a shaped recipe.

❷ The result of this recipe will be a stack of items identified by the ItemStack class and contains an Enderium Block.

❸ This part has two letters: o and e. Each of these letters will represent a different item. The spaces in between the es and next to the o are the empty slots in the recipe.

❹ The letter e is assigned to ender eyes, and the letter o is assigned to obsidian.

Make sure to import everything before launching the game.

These recipes are only examples, so you can feel free to customize them as necessary.

Shapeless Crafting Recipe

Now that you know how to make a shaped recipe, we can move on to shapeless recipes. Shapeless recipes are just like shaped recipes except that they don't require a certain order of blocks/items.

The first shapeless recipe will create nine Ender Ingots from an Enderium Block. To add a shapeless recipe, add the line shown in Example 9-4 to the `init()` method in your main file.

Example 9-4. Shapeless recipe

```
GameRegistry.addShapelessRecipe( ❶
        new ItemStack(enderIngot, 9), ❷
        new ItemStack(enderBlock)); ❸
```

❶ The `addShapelessRecipe()` method adds a shapeless recipe, just like the name says.

❷ The first parameter to this method is the output of the recipe. In this case, nine Ender Ingots will be created.

❸ The second parameter is the input to the recipe. The only `ItemStack` in this recipe will be one Enderium Block.

`ItemStack` is used instead of a regular `Item` or `Block` so that you can specify things like whether the item/block should be enchanted or whether it should be a certain type of item/block. For example, you can't refer to red wool using a regular `Block`; you have to use an `ItemStack` for it.

In the game, the recipe looks like Figure 9-5.

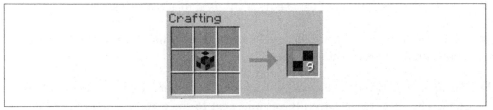

Figure 9-5. Shapeless recipe picture

The Enderium Block can be placed anywhere in the crafting table because this is a shapeless recipe, as shown in Figure 9-6.

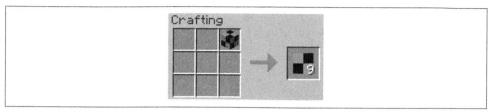

Figure 9-6. Shapeless recipe picture with block in different place

To make a shapeless recipe with more than one item in it, use something like Example 9-5.

Example 9-5. Shapeless recipe with multiple items

```
GameRegistry.addShapelessRecipe( ❶
        new ItemStack(enderIngot, 12),
        new ItemStack(enderBlock, 1),
        new ItemStack(Items.iron_ingot), ❷
        new ItemStack(Items.gold_ingot)); ❸
```

❶ The first part of this method is the same, except that the recipe gives 12 Ender Ingots because you added an Iron Ingot and a Gold Ingot. This way, you can convert Iron Ingots and Gold Ingots into more Ender Ingots.

❷ A shapeless recipe can have up to nine inputs, one for each slot on the crafting table. Each input can be defined as a method parameter. In this case, three input blocks are used.

The first one is similar to Example 9-4. After the `ItemStack` containing the Enderium Block, another `ItemStack` containing an Iron Ingot is added.

❸ One final `ItemStack` containing a Gold Ingot is added to the method.

The recipe should look like Figure 9-7.

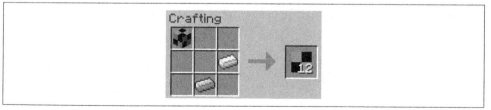

Figure 9-7. Shapeless recipe with multiple items picture

Of course, you need to make sure these recipes produce what they are supposed to by running Minecraft from Eclipse and placing the inputs in a crafting table as they are required.

Again, the items can be put anywhere in the grid.

Smelting Recipe

Smelting recipes produce refined goods.

Smelting is very easy because it requires only one input and one output, plus another parameter for experience. An example of a smelting recipe is shown in Example 9-6.

Example 9-6. New smelting recipe

```
GameRegistry.addSmelting( ❶
        Items.ender_pearl, ❷
        new ItemStack(enderIngot, 1), ❸
        1.0F); ❹
```

❶ The addSmelting() method adds a new smelting recipe.

❷ The first parameter is the input to the recipe and can be either an item or a block. In this case, it is an Ender Pearl item.

❸ The second parameter is the output of the recipe and has to be an ItemStack, so you could make it give you more than one item per smelt.

❹ The last parameter is the experience given from doing this smelting recipe.

Run Minecraft from Eclipse and verify that your recipe works by placing a furnace, putting fuel in the bottom slot, and putting the input, Ender Pearls, in the top slot. Fuel can be anything that burns, such as coal blocks or wood planks.

A furnace running with this recipe for a while would look like Figure 9-8.

Figure 9-8. New smelting recipe picture

Some examples of other smelting recipes include turning obsidian to bedrock, iron ingot to gold ingot, and coal block to diamond.

Brewing Recipe

The final type of recipe that we'll look at is a brewing recipe. Brewing produces potions that can be used to gain various helpful and harming effects. Brewing recipes require only one line, but that one line requires a value that has many parts. The brewing recipe used here will look like Figure 9-9.

Figure 9-9. New brewing recipe picture

The ingredient in this recipe is cake placed in the top slot, and it is brewing awkward potions into other potions. This recipe is mostly about customization, such as potion effect, tier, and duration. There are many effects that you can make, and a lot of them are explained in the `PotionHelper` class. `PotionHelper` is a Minecraft class that contains string codes for each potion.

The `PotionHelper` class contains many different string values such as `blazePowderEffect` and `gunpowderEffect`, which contain string codes with lots of numbers and operators like + and -.

In your main file's `init()` method, add the code shown in Example 9-7.

Example 9-7. New brewing recipe code

```
Items.cake.setPotionEffect(PotionHelper.blazePowderEffect);
```

Make sure to import the `PotionHelper` class.

This line is adding the blaze powder effect to cake. What that means is that cake now works the same way as blaze powder in a brewing stand. Blaze powder turns awkward potions into strength potions, and now cake will do that as well. You can also try this with the other string values, such as `ghastTearEffect` and `speckledMelonEffect`. They all make different types of potions.

The `blazePowderEffect` string value is set to +0-1-2+3&4-4+13 in `PotionHelper`. The numbers and operators are explained more fully later, and a full list is provided in Table 9-2. If you do not know what a certain value does, such as &, then try experimenting with it.

To customize your potion, you can add string values to make the potion a splash potion, a higher tier, or an extended duration. You can also change the raw string value, but that will be explained later. Some things you can add are shown in Table 9-1. To add the values, we'll use a Java + operator to add two strings together. This is called *concatenating* strings in Java. The string values are shown in Table 9-1.

Table 9-1. Customizing your brewing recipe

Name of customization	String value to add
Extended duration	"+6"
Increased tier	"+5"
Splash potion	"+14"

For example, the potion effect from Example 9-7 with extended duration and splash potion would look like Example 9-8.

Example 9-8. Brewing recipe with customizations

```
Items.cake.setPotionEffect(PotionHelper.blazePowderEffect
       + ❶
       "+6" ❷
       + ❸
       "+14"); ❹
```

❶ The Java + operator is used to add the string produced by `PotionHelper.blaze PowderEffect` and the string value after it.

❷ String from extended duration customization

❸ Uses Java operator to concatenate the extended duration customization string and the splash potion customization string

❹ String for splash potion customization

The values shown in Table 9-1 are the common customizations that people use, but there are other values, ranging from 0 to 15, that change the potion as well. Each of these values does something special when you add or subtract it. A list of what each value does is shown in Table 9-2.

Table 9-2. Brewing stand customization string values list

Number	Description
0	Potion effect
1	Potion effect
2	Potion effect
3	Potion effect
4	Ignored
5	Tier
6	Extended duration
7	Ignored
8	Ignored
9	Ignored
10	Ignored
11	Ignored
12	Ignored
13	Can become splash potion
14	Splash potion
15	Ignored

The first three values work together to form the potion effect. They use + as well as -, so try experimenting with different combinations. To change the values, go into the PotionHelper class and take the raw string values. You can change the operators on those values. Also, the numbers 5, 6, 13, and 14 just need a + sign before them to be activated. The number 5 will increase the tier by 1 when activated.

If, at any time while making brewing recipes, the brewing stand does not work, undo what you modified. Some modifications may make the potion value invalid.

Textures

Next, you will learn how to make textures for your blocks and items. This is how you change the default purple-and-black look of newly created blocks and items to a more pleasant one.

Tools

Creating textures requires you to become familiar with a tool that can create or manipulate images. For example, Windows comes with the Paint tool. Mac does not bundle a prebuilt tool to create images, but several can be downloaded from the App Store. A texture image has a resolution of 16 × 16 (i.e., 16 pixels in block height and 16 in block width). You should make your textures 16 × 16 pixels as well, unless you want really detailed textures. If you decide to make a higher resolution, it must be a multiple of 16, such as 32 × 32, 64 × 64, and so on.

There are several books dedicated to teaching image creation, so we will not attempt to do that. Instead, this section will show you how to take an existing texture and manipulate it.

A great tool for making Minecraft textures is GIMP, which you can get from its downloads page (*http://www.gimp.org/downloads/*). This book will not provide an overview or instructions on how to use GIMP, as there are extensive tutorials for using the tool on the GIMP tutorials page (*http://www.gimp.org/tutorials/*). GIMP is a good tool because it contains many ways to color/paint your images and it also can zoom in enough to make the texture easily visible.

An easy way to make Minecraft textures is to import an existing texture and modify it. An easy way to modify textures is by using the Colorify tool under the Colors menu. This tool can tint an image with a certain color. GIMP's Colorify tutorial (*http://docs.gimp.org/en/plug-in-colorify.html*) provides more details about this tool.

The Zoom tool is used to change the zoom level of your working image. You can learn more about this tool by reviewing GIMP's Zoom tutorial (*http://docs.gimp.org/en/gimp-tool-zoom.html*). This tool is important because most Minecraft textures are 16 × 16 pixels, which is a very small size. This tool allows you to zoom the image and work with it comfortably.

Some premade textures are available on Aditya's GitHub page (*http://bit.ly/1xguLEJ*). To download the textures, go to either the *blocks/* or the *items/* folder, and find *enderBlock.png* for the block or *enderIngot.png* for the item. Click the correct file, and you should see a picture of it. Right-click the picture and select Save Image As… to download it onto your computer. Then, you can move it to the correct folder, which will be explained later in this chapter. Don't change the filename while saving it.

These textures are based on a redstone block and an iron ingot. If you are making your own textures, make sure that for the item part, everything that is not the item is transparent. If you make it white instead of transparent, the item will look like a white square with the actual item inside it.

You cannot make transparency with the default imaging tools, but GIMP has a way to make transparent colors. Select the area you want to color transparent, usually the white area around the item. To select the area, you can use the Fuzzy Select tool, which is shown as ✎. Click the white area, and it will select everything that is the same color as the area you clicked. Then go to the Colors menu and select "Color to Alpha". This will make your entire selection transparent.

Images

In order for Forge to pick up your textures and make them visible to Minecraft, they need to be placed in a specific directory. Let's create that directory:

1. Using Windows Explorer on Windows or Finder on Mac, navigate to the folder in which the *lang/* directory was created and the *en_US.lang* file was added. This was done in "Naming Your Block" on page 88. The directory should be called *mymods/*. Make sure it is all lowercase letters, because Forge looks for the directory name you give in lowercase letters.

   This name is important because it is the first part of the texture names, like `mymods:enderBlock` for the block in "Creating the Block Class" on page 85 and `mymods:enderIngot` for the item in "Creating the Item Class" on page 97. This tells Forge that the textures will be located in a folder called *textures/* that is inside this *mymods/* folder.

2. In the *mymods/* folder, create a folder called *textures/*. Forge will look here for any textures that start with `mymods:`.

3. In the *textures/* folder, create two new folders called *blocks/* and *items/*. These will store block and item textures, respectively.

4. In the *blocks/* folder, put your block textures, and in the *items/* folder, put your item textures.

 If you downloaded the textures from GitHub, *enderBlock.png* goes in the *blocks/* folder, and *enderIngot.png* goes in the *items/* folder.

Once you put the textures in the correct folder, rename the textures to the name you gave to `GameRegistry` when you registered the block/item. For example, for the block, the texture name is `enderBlock`, because that was the second parameter (the name) you gave of the `registerBlock()` method of `GameRegistry`. Rename the block texture image to *enderBlock* and the item texture image to *enderIngot*. Minecraft uses only files with the *.png* extension, so make sure the texture files are *.png* files and not *.jpeg* or *.gif* or something else.

Once you have made all of these folders and files, your *src/main/resources* folder should look like Figure 9-10.

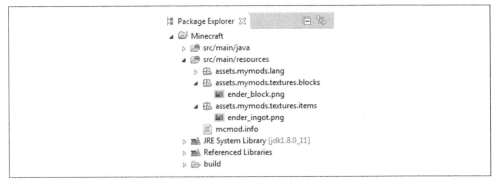

Figure 9-10. Directory structure with textures

Files

Now that you have made the texture image, we will need to make some more files. There are four of these files:

Blockstate file
> Tells Forge which block model to use, depending on which direction the block was placed in

Block model file
> Defines the shape of the block, as well as the texture for each side

`ItemBlock` *model file*
> Defines how the block looks when it is in the player's inventory

Item model file
> Tells Forge what the item should look like

First, you will need to make some new directories. In the *src/main/resources/assets/ mymods* directory, make two new directories called *blockstates* and *models*. In the *models* directory, make two more directories, called *block* and *item*. The *blockstates* directory will store the blockstate file, the *models/block* directory will store the block model, and *models/item* will store the `ItemBlock` and item model files. Your *src/main/ resources* folder should now look like Figure 9-11.

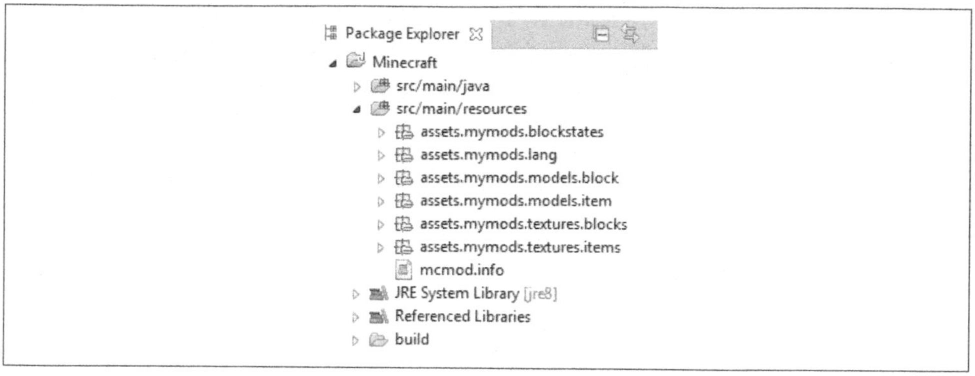

Figure 9-11. Directory structure with blockstates and models folders

First, we will make the blockstate file. Go to your *blockstates* directory and make a new text document without a name. Add the text shown in Example 9-9.

Example 9-9. Blockstate file text

```
{
        "variants": { ❶
                "normal": { "model": "mymods:enderBlock" } ❷
        }
}
```

❶ `"variants"` is used to tell Forge which model to use based on the block direction. Here, the only model is the `enderBlock`, which you will make later. This model will be used regardless of the block direction, but other blocks may have more than one for different directions. For example, a torch has a straight model if it is on the ground, but a different model on the wall.

❷ The word `normal` shows that this texture is for any direction. The words inside the brackets show that the model used will be in the *models/block* directory, and that it will be called `enderBlock`.

Save this file as *enderBlock.json*, because Forge uses JSON files for blockstates and models. The name has to be whatever you gave as the second parameter of `GameRegis try`'s `registerBlock()` when you registered your new block.

 JSON files are like text files, and end with the *.json* extension. They are a simple and intuitive way to organize data.

Now that the blockstate file is done, we need to make the model files. Go to your *models/block* directory and make a new text document. Just like before, don't save it yet. In the new text file, add the code shown in Example 9-10.

Example 9-10. Block model file text

```
{
        "parent": "block/cube", ❶
        "textures": { ❷
                "down": "mymods:blocks/enderBlock",
                "up": "mymods:blocks/enderBlock",
                "north": "mymods:blocks/enderBlock",
                "south": "mymods:blocks/enderBlock",
                "west": "mymods:blocks/enderBlock",
                "east": "mymods:blocks/enderBlock",
                "particle": "mymods:blocks/enderBlock"
        }
}
```

❶ This line tells Forge that this block will be cube-shaped and the same size as a normal block.

❷ The textures given here are for all six faces, one each for down, up, north, south, west, and east direction. There is one more texture for particles as well. If you want, you can use other textures for the different faces. You could make more texture images and use them here to make the block look cooler.

Save this file as *enderBlock.json*, just like the file before.

The last file you need to make for the block is the `ItemBlock` model file. This file is the one that shows how the block will look in the inventory and when it is dropped on the ground. Go to your *models/item* directory and make a new text file. In the file, add the text shown in Example 9-11.

Example 9-11. ItemBlock model file text

```
{
        "parent": "mymods:block.enderBlock", ❶
        "display": { ❷
                "thirdperson": {
                        "rotation": [ 10, -45, 170 ], ❸
                        "translation": [ 0, 1.5, -2.75 ], ❹
                        "scale": [ 0.375, 0.375, 0.375 ] ❺
                }
        }
}
```

❶ This line makes the `ItemBlock` look exactly like the actual block.

❷ This part of the text, including all the indented text, makes the item the right size and location.

❸ The item is rotated so that it looks like other `ItemBlocks` in third-person view.

❹ The item is moved to the player's hand position.

❺ The item is scaled down in size so that it is smaller than the actual block.

Save this file as—you guessed it—*enderBlock.json*.

Now we will make the last file, which is the item model file. Go to your *models/item* directory and make a new text file. Add in the text shown in Example 9-12.

Example 9-12. Item model file text

```
{
    "parent": "builtin/generated", ❶
    "textures": {
        "layer0": "mymods:items/enderIngot" ❷
    },
    "display": { ❸
        "thirdperson": {
            "rotation": [ -90, 0, 0 ],
            "translation": [ 0, 1, -3 ],
            "scale": [ 0.55, 0.55, 0.55 ]
        },
        "firstperson": {
            "rotation": [ 0, -135, 25 ],
            "translation": [ 0, 4, 2 ],
            "scale": [ 1.7, 1.7, 1.7 ]
        }
    }
}
```

❶ This tells Forge that this item model is like any other normal item model.

❷ The texture used here is in the *textures/items* directory and is called *enderIngot*.

❸ These lines tweak the item appearance to make it look better.

Save this file as *enderIngot.json*, because as with the block, you have to give it the name that you gave to `GameRegistry`.

Your *src/main/resources/* directory should now look like Figure 9-12.

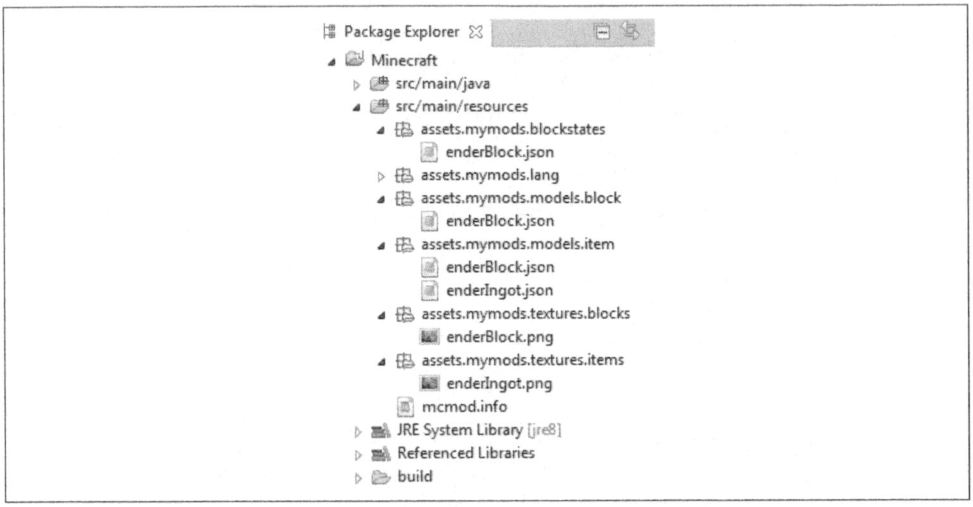

Figure 9-12. Directory structure with blockstate, model, texture, and lang file

Register and Verify the Textures

Now you are almost done making your new textures. The only thing left is to add some code into the `init()` method of your main file. The code is shown in Example 9-13, and is used to tell Forge which models are used for rendering the item/block in the inventory.

Example 9-13. Registering inventory item models

```
Item enderBlockItem = GameRegistry.findItem("mymods", "enderBlock"); ❶
ModelResourceLocation enderBlockModel =
        new ModelResourceLocation("mymods:enderBlock", "inventory"); ❷
Minecraft.getMinecraft().getRenderItem().getItemModelMesher()
        .register(enderBlockItem, 0, enderBlockModel); ❸

Item enderIngotItem = GameRegistry.findItem("mymods", "enderIngot"); ❹
ModelResourceLocation enderIngotModel =
        new ModelResourceLocation("mymods:enderIngot", "inventory");
Minecraft.getMinecraft().getRenderItem().getItemModelMesher()
        .register(enderIngotItem, 0, enderIngotModel);
```

❶ This line finds the `ItemBlock` for the new block by using its name as given to `GameRegistry`.

❷ A new `ModelResourceLocation` is made to store the location of the `ItemBlock` model file.

❸ The `ItemBlock` model file is added to Minecraft's item rendering system so that it is rendered properly.

❹ The same thing is done for the new item.

Make sure to import everything, and once you do, you are done making your textures!

The block and item with the texture on the GitHub link look like Figure 9-13. The item is in an item frame so you can see it easily.

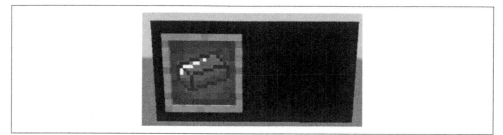

Figure 9-13. Block and item textures in the game

If you want, to make cool-looking textures, you can download textures from the Internet and scale them down to a good size. That way, if you want to make a mod similar to an existing one, you can download the textures instead of making them from scratch.

Summary

In this chapter, you learned about how to make the finishing touches to your mod: recipes and textures. First, you started with recipes, and you learned there are shaped, shapeless, smelting, and brewing recipes. You also learned how to make each kind of recipe. Next, you learned about textures and how Forge has a process to put texture images in the right place. Feel free to create different recipes or modify existing textures to make your mods more appealing.

In the next and final chapter, you will learn about how you can share your mods and install them on your Minecraft client.

CHAPTER 10

Sharing Mods

The previous chapters showed how to create a wide variety of mods. Now that you know how to make mods, it's time to share them with your friends. This can be easily done by packaging these mods into one JAR file. This chapter will show how to share Forge mods. Then, you will learn how to install Minecraft Forge onto your regular Minecraft client so that you can install your mods there. Making the JAR file requires only one command, and installing Forge is also easy. Consequently, this chapter will be short, but useful if you want to share your mods with your friends.

Building the JAR File

Any mods created using Forge need to be properly packaged before they can be shared. This allows Forge to load the mods correctly. Proper packaging is required no matter what the mod is like.

Fortunately, Forge comes with a simple command to package your mods. Open up Command Prompt on Windows or Terminal on Mac, and go to your Forge folder. In that folder, run the command `gradlew build` if you are on a Windows computer or `./gradlew build` if you are on a Mac computer. This command will give the output shown in Example 10-1.

Example 10-1. Gradlew build command output

```
****************************
 Powered By MCP:
 http://mcp.ocean-labs.de/
 Searge, ProfMobius, Fesh0r,
 R4wk, ZeuX, IngisKahn, bspkrs
 MCP Data version : unknown
****************************
```

```
:compileApiJava UP-TO-DATE
:processApiResources UP-TO-DATE
:apiClasses UP-TO-DATE
:sourceMainJava
:compileJava
warning: [options] bootstrap class path not set in conjunction with -source 1.6
Note: Recompile with -Xlint:deprecation for details.
Note: Some input files use unchecked or unsafe operations.
Note: Recompile with -Xlint:unchecked for details.
1 warning
:processResources UP-TO-DATE
:classes
:jar
:compileTestJava UP-TO-DATE
:processTestResources UP-TO-DATE
:testClasses UP-TO-DATE
:test UP-TO-DATE
:extractMcpData UP-TO-DATE
:getVersionJson
:extractUserDev UP-TO-DATE
:genSrgs SKIPPED
:reobf
:assemble
:check UP-TO-DATE
:build

BUILD SUCCESSFUL
```

The exact output of the command may differ based upon your exact JDK version.

This will package your mod into a JAR file, using every single new file you have made. If you don't want to include some of the files in the mod, either delete them or install a new Eclipse and create only the files you want there.

After that is done, navigate to the *build\libs* directory in your Forge folder. You should see a JAR file called *modid-1.0.jar*. This is the default filename generated by Forge. Change this name to whatever you want and share it with your friends.

You can share your JAR file in many ways. You can use email, GitHub, Skype, or any other service that allows you to transfer or store files.

Installing Minecraft Forge on Your Client

Now that you have a mod JAR file, you need a place to install it. This place will be made by installing Minecraft Forge on your client. Go to the Minecraft Forge down-loads page (*http://files.minecraftforge.net/*) to download the installer.

There will be a box like the one shown in Figure 1-1. Change the value to 1.8. The page should now look like the one shown in Figure 1-2.

The latest version of Forge at the time of of writing this book is 1.8. This version might change by the time this book is published or you are reading this book. So select the appropriate version accordingly.

Scroll down on the page until you reach the 1.8 Downloads section. In that section, find the version of Forge you downloaded at the beginning of the book. Instead of clicking Src, click Installer-Win if you are on a Windows computer or Installer if you are on a Mac computer. This will lead you to an AdFly page. Wait for five seconds and then click Skip Ad in the upper-right corner to download the file.

This file is the one that will be used to install Minecraft Forge on your Minecraft client. It will install Forge libraries that are required to run mods, and will also create a new profile on your launcher for this modded version.

Once it is downloaded, run the installer by double-clicking the file. Select Install Client, as shown in Figure 10-1.

Figure 10-1. Installing Forge to your client

After a few minutes, the program will finish and you will have successfully installed Minecraft Forge. When you launch your Minecraft launcher, use the drop-down menu in the lower-left corner to switch to the Forge profile, as shown in Figure 10-2. Then, click the Play button to launch Minecraft with whatever mods you have installed.

Figure 10-2. Switching to the Forge profile

To add mods to your game, first download the mod from the Internet. Then, you will have to navigate to a certain directory depending on whether you are on a Windows or a Mac computer.

If you are on a Windows computer, put it in the *AppData\Roaming\.minecraft\mods* directory.

If you are on a Mac computer, put it in the *Library\Application Support\minecraft \mods* directory.

If you cannot find either of these folders, open up your Minecraft launcher. Click the Edit Profile button in the lower-left corner. A new window will pop up. Click the Open Game Dir button in the lower-right corner. This will take you to the correct folder.

Copy and paste your mod into the folder that you navigated to. Then, run Minecraft using the Forge profile. If your mod doesn't work, then it is either conflicting with another mod or you didn't install other mods required for the mod to work. If that is the case, refer to the mod's page for installation instructions.

Cool Mods That You Can Install

Now that you know how to install mods to Minecraft, this section will give you a list of cool mods that you can install. They are shown in Table 10-1. The mod's name, description, and download link are provided. The links might be out of date, so make sure you always look for a newer link if the one provided does not seem updated.

Table 10-1. Cool mods

Name	Description	Download link
Thaumcraft	Thaumcraft is a mod about magic, where you can draw magic from natural sources and reshape it to perform miracles. You can research items, blocks, and entities using a Thaumometer, and then combine the aspects you get to discover new ways to use magic.	*http://bit.ly/1GUbDwk*
IndustrialCraft2	This mod is more on the tech side of things, adding machines like Miners and Mass Fabricators to automate normal Minecraft tasks like mining and gathering resources.	*http://bit.ly/1BmyixA*
Buildcraft	Buildcraft is another tech mod, but is used more for different things than IndustrialCraft2. It includes quarries to mine out large areas, automated crafting tables so you can build huge factories, and pipes for versatile item transport.	*http://bit.ly/1GUbNE1*

Name	Description	Download link
Forestry for Minecraft	Forestry for Minecraft is a mod that mixes tech and a bit of other aspects together. You can make machines powered by engines, and you can also breed trees or bees at the same time. If you want a mod that is about technology, but with some other things mixed in, Forestry for Minecraft is a good mod to try out. It also has some add-ons, downloaded separately, that add more trees, more bees, and other things.	*http://bit.ly/1NfECMV*
Pixelmon	Pixelmon is basically Pokémon in Minecraft. You can get a starter Pokémon, train it against other wild Pokémon, and become the best trainer around. You can also go on adventures to find legendary Pokémon or shrines to other Pokémon.	*http://bit.ly/1y6eQUC*
Lycanite's Mobs	Lycanite's Mobs adds a whole bunch of cool mobs that spawn all over the place. You can kill the mobs to get items or find underwater temples to get magical scepters. These scepters can do lots of cool stuff, like summoning lightning or shooting out fireballs.	*http://bit.ly/1HDCOvq*
Millénaire	Millénaire makes villages that are vastly better than regular NPC villages. While the only thing that regular villagers can do is trade things for emeralds, Millénaire villagers can build giant structures, trade for a form of currency called deniers, and follow you around to kill any hostile mobs they see. They even have cultures, such as Japanese, Hindu, and Mayan.	*http://bit.ly/1ESVhUA*

As stated before, some of these mods might conflict with other mods. Also, some of them have add-ons that you can download to increase their value. For example, the Extra Bees add-on for Forestry for Minecraft adds tons of different bees that can produce copper, rubber, and many other items.

Summary

In this chapter, you learned how to package your mod into a JAR file with a simple command. Then, you learned where your mods folder is. You can put any number of mods in the folder, but beware of lag. Also, some mods might conflict with each other.

This chapter ends the modding part of this book. After this will be a few appendixes with useful information to learn more. Now that you know how to make a mod and share it, the only limit is your imagination.

Happy modding!

What Is Minecraft?

This appendix is an introduction to the game of Minecraft, and is aimed toward readers who have not played the game. If you do play the game, you can skip this appendix, because you most likely know the content of this chapter well. If not, you may want to read it so you know what the game is all about. All these topics are explained in greater detail at the official Minecraft wiki (*http://minecraft.gamepedia.com/Mine craft_Wiki*), but this is a more concise introduction to the game. The wiki is typically the biggest source of information for *Minecrafters*, players involved in the game of Minecraft.

So, are you ready to be a Minecrafter?

Minecraft is a 3D game about breaking and placing *blocks* to obtain *materials*. These materials can then be used to build or *craft* new *items* and *tools*. These, in turn, can be used to harvest more types of blocks. The game also contains *entities*, which are dynamic moving objects in Minecraft (e.g., cows, pigs, and horses). Entities that are hostile are called *monsters* (e.g., zombies and creepers). *Bosses* are monsters that are very hard to defeat.

Other activities in the game include exploration, gathering resources, crafting, and combat.

Players can travel to different *worlds*, or *dimensions* in gamespeak. The game contains three dimensions:

- The Overworld
- The Nether
- The End

The *Overworld* is like a normal wilderness on Earth. It has grass, trees, villages, and other normal things you might find out in nature. The *Nether* is like a big cave system, and it is covered with lava and fire. Lots of hostile mobs spawn there, which makes it that much more dangerous. The *End* is the final dimension, and it is like a floating island. The island is made of End Stone and has obsidian pillars on top. This dimension contains one of Minecraft's bosses, the *Ender Dragon*.

The game is played on a *map*, which is a certain arrangement of blocks that defines how the world looks. When a world is generated, it creates a *seed* that defines what the map looks like. The seed can also be specified during world creation. If the same seed is used for two worlds, they will look exactly the same. You can also download maps made by other people and play on them.

Each player has his own *inventory*, which contains his blocks, items, and armor.

An important part to understand about Minecraft is that there is no "finishing" the game. The player can move between dimensions and build structures however she wants.

Downloading the Game and Registering an Account

Minecraft was written by Markus "Notch" Persson and is now maintained by Mojang. In order to download the game, you need to create an account on Mojang. If you already have an account, you can skip this step. You can use your Mojang account to log in to Minecraft. To register, go to *http://minecraft.net/*. Click the orange button on the right that says Get Minecraft to go to the registration page, as shown in Figure A-1.

Registering an account requires you to enter your email and a password. Click Create Account to continue, as shown in Figure A-2.

Get Minecraft
26.95 USD
or play the demo
Already bought the game?
Download it here

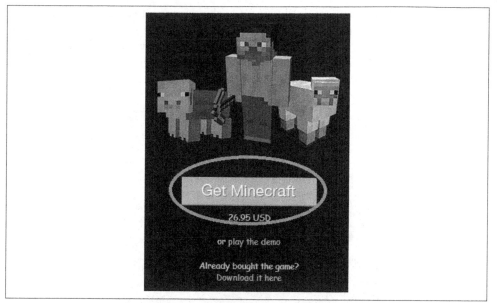

Figure A-1. Registering a Mojang account

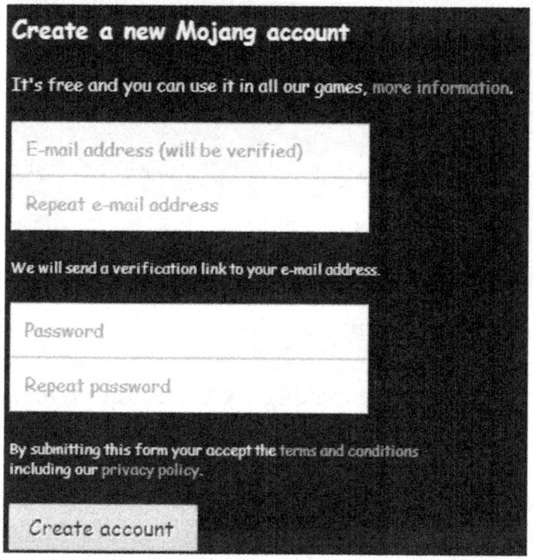

Create a new Mojang account
It's free and you can use it in all our games, more information.
E-mail address (will be verified)
Repeat e-mail address
We will send a verification link to your e-mail address.
Password
Repeat password
By submitting this form your accept the terms and conditions
including our privacy policy.
Create account

Figure A-2. Minecraft registration page

Follow the prompts that appear until you get to the terms and conditions. Look over them and agree to them to continue. You will then reach a page that prompts you to buy the game. The cost is $26.95. You must buy the game to try the samples explained in this book. The buying page is shown in Figure A-3. Enter all the required information and buy the game to continue.

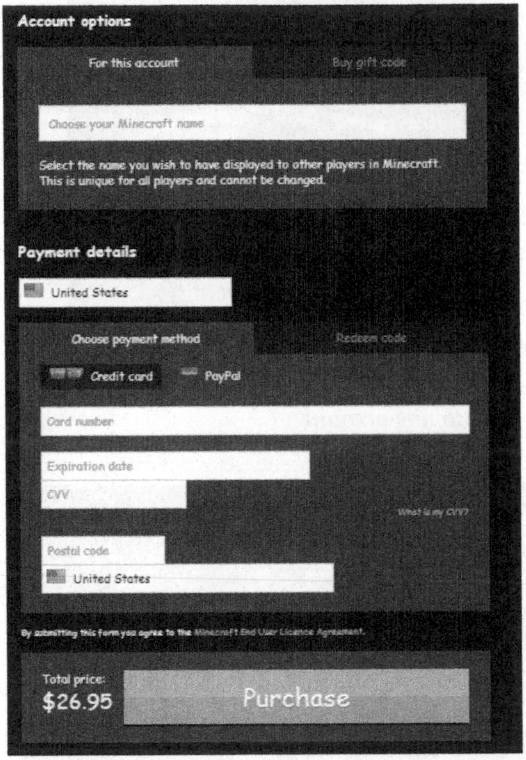

Figure A-3. Buying a Minecraft account

When you buy an account, you are making your account *premium*. You can have an account that is not premium, but you cannot use it to log into the game. Basically, you cannot do very much with a nonpremium account. After making the account premium, you will see a download page. This page is for downloading the *launcher*, which is the program that launches the game. The download page will look different for each operating system. A Windows version of the page is shown in Figure A-4.

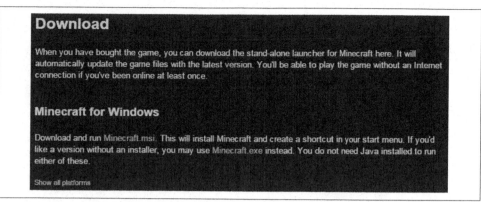

Figure A-4. Downloading the launcher

You can click the "Show all platforms" button to see download options for each operating system. Download the one you need, and run it by double-clicking its icon. You should get a screen similar to Figure A-5.

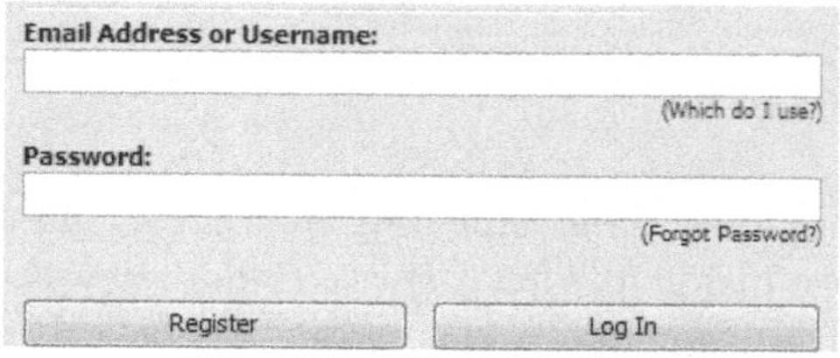

Figure A-5. Launcher login

Enter the account credentials used to purchase the game and click Log In.

Starting the Game

Starting the game takes you to the launcher screen, shown in Figure A-6, which allows you to launch the game. You can make *profiles*, which are different ways to launch the game. For example, you can have one profile for the newest version and one for the older version. Click New Profile to make a new profile.

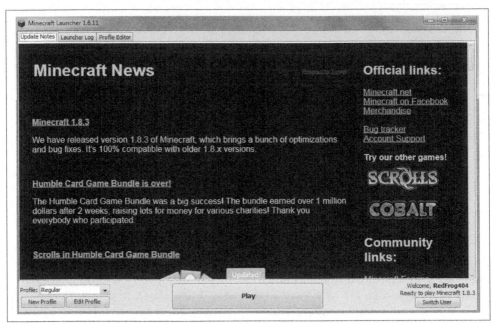

Figure A-6. Launcher screen

Click Play to launch the game. If the launching works, you should see a window pop up with a MOJANG logo inside it. After a few seconds, a new screen will pop up that looks like Figure A-7. This is the main game screen.

Figure A-7. Minecraft game screen

The game has a *client* and a *server* component. The server stores the world and its entities, items, and blocks. This allows the game to be played in *singleplayer* mode, where a player connects to a server using a client and plays the game. Alternatively, multiple players, using different clients across different machines, can connect to a server and play with each other collaboratively. This is called *multiplayer* mode. An internal server is automatically started for singleplayer mode. No other players can join this server. A server has to be started externally for multiplayer mode.

To start the game in singleplayer mode, click Singleplayer to get to the singleplayer screen shown in Figure A-8. By default, no worlds exist, so one needs to be created before you can play.

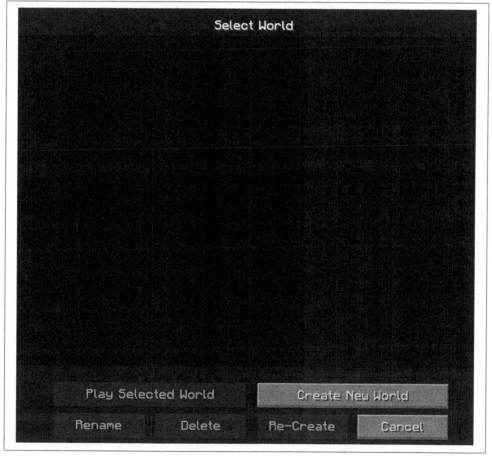

Figure A-8. Minecraft singleplayer screen

Click Create New World to create a new world from the screen shown in Figure A-9.

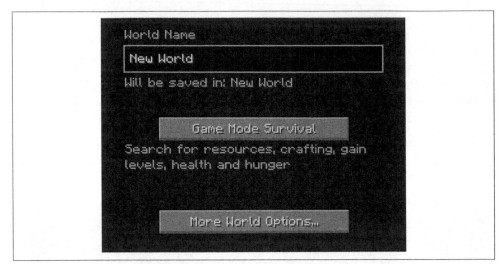

Figure A-9. Create a new world

You can change the world name and game mode here.

The world name can be changed by clicking the New World box. Type the name of your new world here.

The game can be played in five game modes:

Survival
Requires players to acquire resources and gain experience points, and maintain their *health* and *hunger*. Players die when they run out of health. If a player is in survival, creative, or spectator mode, the player will respawn.

Creative
Players have an unlimited supply of resources, the ability to fly, and no health or hunger. This means the player never dies in the game.

Hardcore
Same as survival, respawning is disabled and so the map is deleted upon the player's death. The game is also set to a difficulty of hard, so mobs do a lot more damage and the player loses hunger very fast.

Spectator
Same as creative, but you have a survival inventory and are invisible. You can also pass through blocks like a ghost. You can also see the world from a mob's perspective. You cannot start a world in spectator mode; it has to be achieved in the game.

Adventure

The same as survival mode, but the player cannot break any blocks besides weak blocks like glass and glowstone.

To change your world's game mode, click the Game Mode button, shown in Figure A-10. Creative mode is the easiest game mode to start with.

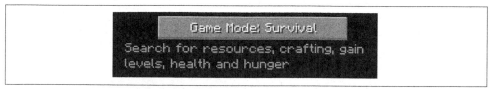

Figure A-10. Change Minecraft game mode

The button will change its text to match the game mode that is chosen.

You can also click More World Options… to configure more options about your world. These include whether there are cheats, a bonus chest (with materials to start you off), and more.

The game allows modifications (known as *mods*) that can change certain aspects of how the game was originally written. These mods can add content to the game to alter gameplay. For example, new blocks, mobs, and abilities of player can be added. This entire book is about creating these mods.

It's very common to have a server run with multiple mods. There are almost an infinite number of mods someone could do to make Minecraft a more amusing game to play. There is no official API to create these mods, but there are several third-party vendors that provide that capability; Minecraft Forge is one such API. The ability to write mods and alter the gameplay gives players more control over the game and gets them more excited.

The remainder of this chapter explains key components of the game.

Blocks

Minecraft worlds are made entirely of *blocks*. Some blocks are realistic, like wood, dirt, mycelium, and pumpkins. On the other hand, some blocks are fictional, like soul sand, nether brick, end stone, and block of diamond. If Minecraft was like reality, each block would be one cubic meter. Because each block is so big, Minecraft worlds can be bigger than Earth. To place a block, right-click the ground. To destroy a block, left-click the block you want to destroy. Some blocks have special capabilities like creating light, blowing up, and being transparent. Usually, grass is at the top of all Minecraft worlds, with dirt and stone underneath. Some blocks, called *ores*, can be found scattered around the stone. These blocks range from coal to diamonds to emeralds.

Not all blocks are 1 × 1 × 1 meters. Some blocks, called *slabs*, are half the size of normal blocks because they are half as tall. Other blocks, like trapdoors and carpets, are even shorter. Some small blocks have special capabilities. Some examples include signs (which can be written on), ladders (which can be climbed on), and fences (which normally can't be jumped over).

Figure A-11 shows some different types of blocks.

Figure A-11. Different types of blocks

The blue background is made of lapis lazuli blocks. The blocks in the top row are all types of wood. The blocks in the bottom are all variants of stone. Note that this example does not show all of the possible Minecraft blocks.

Items

Items in Minecraft are based on real-world items: diamonds, seeds, glass bottles, and more. Items cannot be placed, but you can interact with them in several ways:

- Some items, like clocks and compasses, change texture depending on the time or where you are facing, respectively.
- Other items, like apples and pumpkin pie, can be eaten to restore hunger so your player doesn't die of starvation.
- Some items, like seeds and potatoes, can be planted on dirt to provide more of its type.

Figure A-12 shows different items. Again, the blue background is made of lapis lazuli blocks.

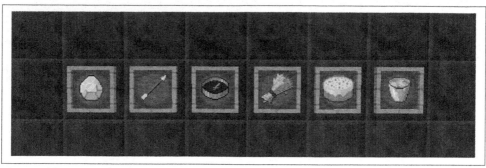

Figure A-12. Different types of items

The items shown in Figure A-12 include (in order from left to right) diamond, arrow, compass, wheat, cake, and lava bucket. Again, this is just a small sampling of the items in Minecraft—there are many more.

Transforming Blocks and Items

In Minecraft, there are many ways to transform items/blocks into other items/blocks. The main methods to achieve this are crafting, smelting, and brewing.

Crafting

The most common way to transform items into other items is called *crafting*. To craft an item or block, you must first craft a crafting table. When you open up your inventory, you will see a 2 × 2 grid. This is called the *minicrafting grid*, as shown in Figure A-13.

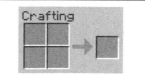

Figure A-13. Minicrafting grid

Minecraft has a predefined set of *crafting recipes*. To craft an item, put the ingredients defined by the recipe in the grid and a *result item* will appear on the right. For example, to craft a crafting table, place a wood log in any of the slots, as shown in Figure A-14. This will give you four wood planks that can then be added to your inventory.

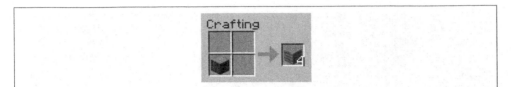

Figure A-14. Crafting wooden planks

Fill up the minicrafting grid with planks, as shown in Figure A-15, to receive one crafting table.

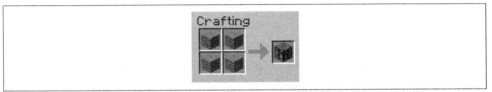

Figure A-15. Crafting a crafting table

If you change the placement of the items, you may not be able to craft the item you are looking to craft. For this reason, it is important to know how to craft basic items such as a crafting table. The crafting table can be right-clicked to open a GUI that contains a grid like the minicrafting grid in your inventory. The only difference is that the crafting table grid is 3 × 3, as shown in Figure A-16, while the minicrafting grid is 2 × 2. The crafting table unlocks many new recipes such as chests, pistons, and others.

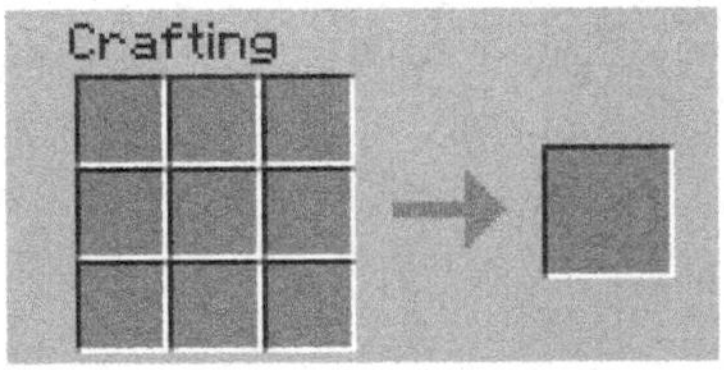

Figure A-16. Crafting table GUI

Another important thing about crafting is that some recipes are shaped, so you have to put items in a certain way, but some items are shapeless, so you can put certain items in any way you want. For example, the recipe for a chest is shaped, but the recipe for wooden planks is shapeless.

All crafting recipes are explained in detail on the Crafting page of the official Minecraft wiki (*http://minecraft.gamepedia.com/Crafting*).

Smelting

The next way to turn items into other items is called *smelting*. Smelting an item can be achieved through crafting a furnace by placing cobblestone, as shown in Figure A-17. Smelting takes 10 seconds to finish, and the smelted item is then added to your inventory.

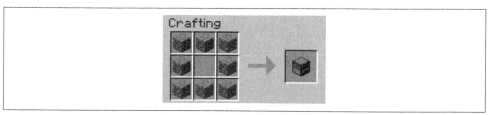

Figure A-17. Crafting a furnace

Placing the furnace in your world and right-clicking it will open the GUI shown in Figure A-18.

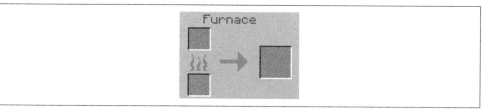

Figure A-18. The furnace GUI

This GUI has four parts:

- The top slot is for the item/block that you want to smelt.
- The bottom slot is for fuel that will power the furnace.
- The slot on the right will contain the smelted product once the smelting is done.
- The arrow shows the smelting progress.

Some examples of items that can be smelted are as follows:

- Sand into glass
- Raw chicken into cooked chicken
- Iron ore into iron ingot

Some examples of fuel are as follows:

- Coal (8 operations)
- Wooden plank (1.5 operations)
- Sapling (0.5 operations)

Figure A-19 shows how a raw chicken can be smelted into cooked chicken.

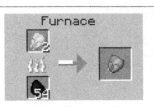

Figure A-19. Smelting raw chicken into cooked chicken

All smelting recipes are explained in detail on the Smelting page of the official Mine-craft wiki (*http://minecraft.gamepedia.com/Smelting*).

Brewing

The last main way to transform items is called *brewing*, which lets you create potions. Brewing takes 20 seconds to finish. To brew potions, you must first craft a *brewing stand* using cobblestone and a blaze rod, as shown in Figure A-20.

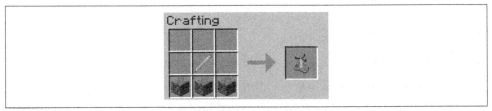

Figure A-20. Crafting a brewing stand

Placing the brewing stand in your world and right-clicking it will open a GUI, as shown in Figure A-21.

Figure A-21. Brewing stand GUI

The top slot is for an ingredient, and the bottom slot is for water bottles or potions that you are going to modify. As with the furnace, the arrow shows the progress. The bubbles on the left are just for decoration. The most important potion is called an *awkward potion*. You can create this potion by putting water bottles in the bottom slots and a *nether wart* in the top slot, as shown in Figure A-22.

Figure A-22. Creating awkward potions

From this potion, you can create many other potions. For example, using a *golden carrot* in an awkward potion gives you a potion of *night vision*. Also, using *glowstone dust* in a potion will increase its *potency*, while using *redstone* will increase its duration. The effects given by glowstone and redstone do not increase when you use more, and you cannot have increased potency and increased duration at the same time. Some more examples of potions you can brew are as follows:

- Magma cream on an awkward potion for Fire Resistance
- Blaze powder on an awkward potion for Strength
- A fermented spider eye on a water bottle for Weakness

You can put one, two, or three water bottles/potions in the bottom slots—it doesn't matter. All of them will have the same effect.

All brewing recipes are explained in detail on the Brewing page of the official Minecraft wiki (*http://minecraft.gamepedia.com/Brewing*).

Mobs

Mobs in Minecraft are like animals in the real world. For example, cows, sheep, pigs, and chickens exist in the game, just as in real life. There are also fictional characters like creepers, zombies, and skeletons. Mobs have artificial intelligence (AI), so they can move around. Different mobs also drop different items when killed. Some mobs can do special things like jump over gaps or shoot arrows using bows. Some mobs can even fly and shoot explosives!

Figure A-23 shows some examples of mobs.

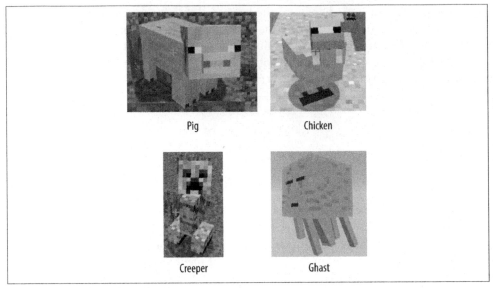

Pig   Chicken

Creeper   Ghast

Figure A-23. Examples of mobs

Mobs can be spawned with *spawn eggs*. Spawn eggs are items and cannot be legitimately obtained in any game modes other than creative. Each mob's spawn egg has different colors. Otherwise, they all look the same. Also, some mobs are passive, meaning they do not attack you as the player, but some mobs are hostile, meaning they will try to attack you. Some mobs are in the middle, because they are neutral. They will attack you only if you provoke them.

Tools

Tools are items that can break certain blocks or do certain things. There are five main types of tools: swords, pickaxes, axes, shovels, and hoes. There are also some other tools: fishing rods, shears, bows, and flint and steel. The main tools can be made of five materials: gold, wood, stone, iron, and diamond. These are in order from worst to best. The other tools do not have tiers. Gold is not good because it has very low durability, even though it mines fast. Gold tools have only 33 uses. Diamond, on the other hand, mines only a little bit slower, but it has much more durability—about 1,500 uses.

Different tools do different things. For example, swords let you do more damage against mobs than using your fist; hoes let you till dirt for farming; and flint and steel can place blocks of fire and ignite TNT. Figure A-24 shows some of the Minecraft tools.

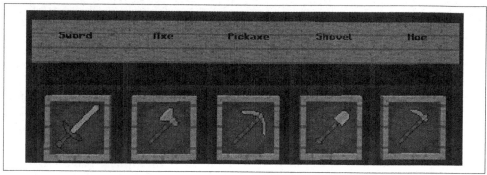

Figure A-24. Minecraft tools

The tools are all in the Diamond tier. Their names are written above them on Sign blocks.

Commands

Another important part of Minecraft is commands. *Commands* can be typed into the game to do special things. For example, the /summon command summons any mob you want it to, wherever you want it to. Another command is /help, which can show you every command in the game and what it does, as shown in Figure A-25.

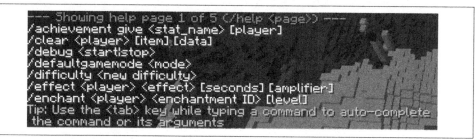

Figure A-25. Output from the /help command

By default, to type in a command, you have to press /. This will open up a bar at the bottom of your screen called the *chat bar*. You can also open this bar by pressing T. Type your command into this bar, and then press Enter to execute it. If the command is not recognized by the game, the following message will be printed:

```
Unknown command. Try /help for a list of commands
```

When creating a world, if you click the More World Options… button in the middle of the screen, you will be taken to a new screen with more options for your world. In this new screen, there will be a button saying Allow Cheats: OFF if you are in survival or hardcore mode, or Allow Cheats: ON if you are in creative mode. Click this button to toggle between cheats and no cheats. If cheats are on, you will have commands like /gamemode to change your game mode and /give to give you items. Without cheats, you will have only some basic commands like /help.

Summary

In this appendix, you learned about the basics of Minecraft. You learned how it has a client and server component, and how they are different. You learned about blocks, items, and mobs, and how they are used. You also learned about tools and commands and what they do. Minecraft includes many other things, like biomes, redstone, enchanting, and farming. You can read about these at the official Minecraft wiki (*http://minecraft.gamepedia.com/Minecraft_Wiki*). This appendix just provides a basic introduction of the game.

Eclipse Shortcuts and Correct Imports

Eclipse Shortcuts

Eclipse is a very powerful tool and includes lots of options for editing Java. These options can be accessed using different menus. However, sometimes clicking menu items for repetitive tasks can be cumbersome or boring, so Eclipse enables some helpful shortcuts that allow you to become a better modder. For example, the Import shortcut can be very useful if you have a lot of classes to import.

Table B-1 provides a handy list of shortcuts (note that there are different shortcuts depending on your platform).

Table B-1. Eclipse shortcuts

Usage	Windows shortcut	Mac shortcut
Save the current file	Ctrl-S	Cmd-S
Import everything	Ctrl-Shift-O	Cmd-Shift-O
Comment the selected text	Ctrl-/	Cmd-/
Uncomment the selected text	Ctrl-/	Cmd-/
Show options for code completion	Ctrl-Space	Control-Space
Quick fix for errors and warnings, depends on the cursor position	Ctrl-1	Control-1
Rename the selected element	Alt-Shift-R	Alt-Cmd-R
Format source code	Ctrl-Shift-F	Control-Shift-F

Usage	Windows shortcut	Mac shortcut
Maximize Java editor	Ctrl-M	Cmd-M
Run Minecraft	Ctrl-F11	Cmd-Fn-F11
Complete list of shortcuts	Ctrl-Shift-L	Cmd-Shift-L

Correct Imports

Different Java packages can have classes with the same name. Obviously, only a class from a particular package will serve the intended purpose for our code. So, when importing classes during mod creation, it's important to pick the right package.

This can be easily done using Ctrl-Shift-O or Cmd-Shift-O in Eclipse. However, there may be multiple classes of the same name but in different packages. There is only one that you should import in all of those cases. Table B-2 shows which import is correct.

Table B-2. Correct imports

Class	Correct import
Entity	`net.minecraft.entity.Entity`
Item	`net.minecraft.item.Item`
Random	`java.util.Random`
Action	`net.minecraftforge.event.entity.player.PlayerInteractEvent.Action`
List	`java.util.List`
Material	`net.mninecraft.block.material.Material`

In all other cases, the class can be imported from one package only.

Downloading the Source Code from GitHub

Source code for the mods created in this book, and for some additional mods, is available at *https://github.com/AdityaGupta1/minecraft-modding-book*. We will keep adding source code for more mods here.

This appendix will teach you how to download the source code for the mods in this book from GitHub. It is especially useful if you have a print copy of this book, because it is easier to download the source code and copy/paste than to type it. It is also useful if you have an error in your code and you don't know how to fix it.

First, go to *https://github.com/AdityaGupta1/minecraft-modding-book*. All of the source code is stored at this link. Then, in the lower-right corner, you should see a Download ZIP button. You might need to scroll down a bit to see it. It should look like Figure C-1.

Figure C-1. Download ZIP button

Click this button to download a ZIP folder containing all of the source code. It should be called *minecraft-modding-book*. Extract the contents of this folder in a directory on your Desktop. Inside this folder, you should see another folder called *minecraft-modding-book-master*. Go inside this folder, and you should see a folder called *src* and a file called *README.asciidoc*. Ignore the *README.asciidoc* file. The *src* folder is the important one.

The folder structure is shown in Figure C-2.

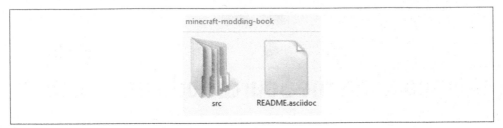

Figure C-2. Unzipped folder from GitHub

The *src* folder contains the Java source code and configuration files for all the mods in this book, and some additional ones as well. You can use any text editor (e.g., Notepad or Sublime Text) to view and copy/paste the source code.

Alternatively, all source code can be copied into your Minecraft Forge folder and the mods can be seen in action right away. For that, open up your Minecraft Forge folder, and delete the *src* folder inside it. Then, copy the *src* folder from the *minecraft-modding-book-master* folder into your Minecraft Forge folder. When you open up Eclipse and launch Minecraft, all of the mods should work correctly.

Devoxx4Kids

By Stephan Janssen

The best way to predict the future is to create it.

—Alan Kay

Minecraft modding is actually one of the Devoxx4Kids (D4K) workshops we teach around the world, kickstarted by Arun Gupta's son. Arun asked me to do a write-up on D4K to provide readers with additional information about this initiative and its background.

In addition to providing an overview of D4K overall, this appendix discusses some of the other exciting D4K workshops we teach and even offer freely on our website (*http://www.devoxx4kids.org*).

In "D4K Best Practices" on page 162, I share some practical details that should help if you decide to start your own local D4K chapter.

How Did D4K Start?

In 2001, after my consultancy company JCS Int. got acquired, I was evaluating what I would do next. At that time, I was already running the Belgian Java User Group (BeJUG) for several years. The opportunity and challenge of organizing a European JavaOne-like conference was something I thought would be exciting to do. From that idea, JavaPolis was born. Fast-forward 13 years (with a rebrand to Devoxx in 2008) and the event has grown into the biggest Java community conference around the world with close to 6,000 developers annually attending Devoxx Belgium, France, and the United Kingdom.

In July 2011, my son Arthur (11 years at that time) surprised me with the following question: "Dad, I want to learn how to program!" (Figure D-1). If you're a developer, you can imagine the impact this had on me: alarm bells and fireworks went off at the same time. I frantically started searching the Web for sites and books that could help me. I was truly shocked by the limited search results I found. Some English material was available, but relevant material in Flemish (11-year-olds in Belgium are not yet fluent in reading English) was almost nonexistent.

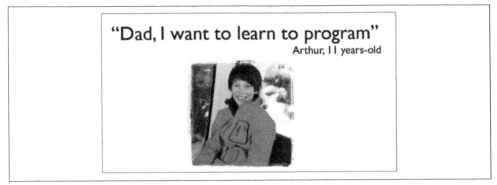

Figure D-1. Arthur Janssen

I did find a book called *Teaching Kids Programming* by Java Champion Yakov Fain, and for a moment I considered translating his work into Dutch. But then the idea struck me: I had been organizing events for many years, so why not organize an event for children? I informed my wife (Kristien) and Arthur that I would start a Devoxx4Kids just for him and he could also invite friends—he was excited. Bonus points for the dad. :)

On February 29, 2012, we organized a Programming for Kids BeJUG evening session (*http://bit.ly/1NfERHT*) where I had invited Tasha Carl (who already had experience with organizing a girls-only event). She also brought an Aldebaran NAO robot, which welcomed everybody and created a special feeling of excitement. We had around 20 people attending, including Daniel De Luca taking pictures, who would eventually lead the worldwide D4K initiative.

Just imagine, the Aldebaran NAO robot could be the Commodore 64 of this generation!

We discussed whether organizing a one-day event would make any difference (actually two events, because we would have one for Flemish and another for French children). Some people were skeptical, and thought this initiative would just be a small water drop on a hot plate, basically only teasing children with a technology cake and then placing it back in the fridge. But I was determined. I had promised my son this would happen, whatever it took. We brainstormed about the possible workshops and soon Scratch, Lego Mindstorms, and a Mars rover were workshops we thought could both inspire the children and motivate the voluntary instructors.

Kristien called some schools whose students attend Devoxx on a regular basis and after a couple of phone calls we had two locations for our very first D4K events—yes!

Two years later, D4K has morphed into a worldwide initiative with chapters all over the world, reaching 2,000 children. Basically every weekend, one or two D4K events are taking place somewhere in the world. The Belgian event had created a snowball effect; of course, showing a really nice D4K video (made by Roy van Rijn) at the opening Devoxx keynote in front of 3,500 developers did help to spread the word and infect other IT parents with this very child-friendly virus!

We even received the Duke's Choice Award at JavaOne San Francisco (Figure D-2). We were receiving great signs that we were doing something right.

Figure D-2. Duke's Choice Award at JavaOne 2013

Why Should Every City Have a D4K Chapter?

Every city in the world should have a D4K chapter, as it can help fill the technology gap among kids.

The Classic Education Is Broken!

More and more teachers are starting to attend the D4K events. Some want to see what they can reuse, while others just want to experience it firsthand and get a reality check of what's available.

Sadly enough, there seems to be a huge discrepancy between what children would like to see at school and what they actually get. Most of the time, teenagers don't go beyond Excel, PowerPoint, and surfing the Web.

The D4K initiative (and many others like this) are leading by example and demonstrating that technology can be fun and enjoyable to teach. You don't need to invest a lot of money in hardware to educate children about the basics of programming, including robotics and even electronics. Just look at the D4K workshops, download them, and get started!

Gender Equality in IT

Every year at Devoxx Belgium, we welcome 3,500 developers, of which only 5% are women. It's really painful to see, and evidenced by the long queues for the men's restroom.

Amazingly enough, at the first D4K event, we had around 75 children and 35% were girls! It seems, at least if we look at the Devoxx ecosystem, that over a period of six to eight years, the ratio of female versus male engineers drops enormously.

I'm convinced that with the D4K movement we can hopefully inspire or at least expose technology to this young Internet generation and maybe even influence some (even if it's only a few) into a technology career. I'm personally looking forward to meeting the first Devoxxian that will approach me and tell me she attended a D4K event and is now pursuing an IT career. Wouldn't that be amazing?!

Demystify Technology

When children see the Aldebaran NAO robot, you see stars in their eyes (the parents are always equally impressed). But after that workshop, you notice that a small part of the magic is vaporized. Many children realize that the magical robot does only what it is told to do—otherwise, nothing happens.

Demystifying technology, electronics, and even robots with children is crucial because understanding more clearly the wonders but also the pitfalls of what lays behind this "plastic" facade of both a robot and websites should be common knowledge. In addition, with the daily exposure to social networks, we need to educate this young generation that without code, these magical things do (almost) nothing.

The D4K Workshops

Our repertoire of D4K workshops is growing year by year, and different D4K groups explore new techniques, programs, and robot-like devices for different age groups. Modding Minecraft is only one of the many popular workshops your child can explore.

Before we have a closer look, a golden rule for workshops geared toward children is that you provide instant gratification. Make sure you start with a nice demo, showing them what they will learn or have them play with the material after a maximum of 10 minutes' introduction. This way, you get the attention from the children and they don't lose focus.

Let's have a closer look.

Scratch

Scratch was developed in 2003 at the MIT Media Lab and made available to the public in 2007. This application allows children to visually learn programming concepts in a fun way (Figure D-3). What I really like about Scratch is that it's free and available in many different languages.

Figure D-3. Kids programming at a workshop

Another super feature of Scratch is that children can publish their "program" online and share it with friends. Not only can their friends and parents see the result, they can also download and clone the "source code" and evolve the program where others have stopped.

The D4K Scratch workshop takes you step by step through the process of exploring and playing with different features. In less than 10 minutes, you can show how the Scratch development environment works, point the children to the examples, and from there, children can explore this fun new world.

You don't need a powerful computer; it even comes preinstalled on a Raspberry Pi, which is only $35. Add a keyboard and screen to the Raspberry Pi and you're ready to get started.

Recently, we've added an extra device to this workshop, named LeapMotion. This device is smaller than a deck of cards and allows you to interact with your Scratch game by moving your hand in the air above the LeapMotion. This is a pretty magical device (even for us adults), and allows children to explore hand commands and more.

Download the Scratch workshop from the D4K website (*http://bit.ly/1LXoPqW*).

Raspberry Pi

The Raspberry Pi (shown in Figure D-4) is really important. If you need a cheap computer for your D4K workshops, then look no further: the Raspberry Pi is *the* solution. We've seen initiatives where schools are starting to replace their old Windows computers with these $35 computer wonders. It even has an HDMI port allowing you to connect to an existing TV and use that as your screen.

Figure D-4. The Raspberry Pi

Raspberry Pi comes preinstalled with Python and Java, opening the door to other free educational software like Greenfoot and Alice—even Scratch comes preinstalled.

Lego Mindstorms

Lego Mindstorms, which are a bit more expensive (approximately $350), are really nice robots (Figure D-5). Children often compare these Lego robots to the Transformers, because they can eventually morph into different shapes and sizes.

One Lego Mindstorms box enables you to build different kinds of robots, where the motor block in combination with the camera module (to detect colored objects) and audio module (to give audio commands, like clapping your hands) provides you almost endless use-cases for a fun workshop.

Figure D-5. Lego Mindstorms robot

We've already explored several workshops. In one, the robot had to move when you placed a blue ball in front of the camera, and when you clapped, the robot arms would close and take the ball, and the robot would turn around and return to the original position. In a less difficult one, the robot uses the camera module to follow a black line that is provided in the box.

Pierre Mistrot has made a really nice Lego Mindstorms workshop (*http://bit.ly/ 1bt52iI*).

The Aldebaran NAO Robot

The star of many D4K events is the child-like Aldebaran NAO robot shown in Figure D-6 (unfortunately, this is an expensive piece of hardware—approximately $3,900 for certified developers). D4K was fortunate enough to receive such a robot during the Devoxx opening keynote in Belgium in 2013. We try to share this robot with as many D4K events as possible, but because this is not a small box, we often personally deliver it at the event.

Because of the price tag, you don't see them that often, which explains why the (tech) parents love to see this robot in action. The NAO robot can play music while dancing, follow an object, walk, grab objects, talk and listen, and much more.

It has a visual development interface called Choreograph that works on both Windows and Mac. You basically drag and drop command icons on a panel and then the robot executes this when you press the Run button.

Figure D-6. The Aldebaran NAO robot

You do need to stress to the children that this is not a toy (or at least that it's a very expensive one). That's why we often have only one in a workshop, so that we can keep an eye on it and children can upload their command storyboards one by one when a robot is available.

Daniel De Luca has made a really nice workshop (*http://bit.ly/1BmyMUs*). In short, you give the robot a ball and tell the robot where to place it.

Arduino

The D4K chapter in the Netherlands (thanks, Roy) created the first Arduino D4K workshop. Roy had ordered some Arduino starter kit boxes, which come with different electronic goodies, including an Arduino and breadboard (Figure D-7).

This workshop starts with the basics of understanding electronics, including concepts like volts, watts, and Ohm's law, but in a child-friendly way with lots of pictures and a simple analogy with water pressure to explain the direction of electricity and transistors.

Figure D-7. An Arduino and breadboard

We start with blinking some LEDs and depending on the age, you can allow the children to only place the electronic parts on the breadboard. With a group of older children, you can even have them write the C application that does the actual blinking of the LED (Example D-1).

The workshop can be downloaded from the D4K website (*http://bit.ly/19PtDgZ*).

Example D-1. Setting an LED in C using an Arduino

```c
long dernierTemps = 0;

long periode = 10000;

int etatLED = LOW;

void setup( ) {
  pinMode(13, OUTPUT);
}

void loop() {

  unsigned long maintenant = millis();

  if (maintenant - dernierTemps > periode) {
    dernierTemps = maintenant;
    if (etatLED == LOW) {
      etatLED = HIGH;
    } else {
      etatLED = LOW;
    }
    digitalWrite(13, etatLED);
  }
}
```

Greenfoot

Greenfoot is a development environment based on the Java programming language and is aimed at teenagers around 12–14 years old. Greenfoot introduces children to object-oriented concepts of classes and objects, inheritance, behavior, and state.

One of the D4K workshops we run involves making a game named Bobby Snake. In the game, when the snake eats more, its tail will become longer and longer.

When Scratch has been mastered, Greenfoot is a great environment to bring your programming skills to a higher level. You still have a visual representation of the playground, but next to it you'll see a graphical representation of your object tree.

D4K Best Practices

This section defines some of the best practices that we've learned over the past couple years of delivering these workshops.

Location

First, you need to find a location for your event, preferably a school that has some computer rooms. Just show the D4K promo movies and website to the school's administrators and often that will be enough to get them excited. Schools love to be associated with these initiatives. Make sure to invite the teachers—this way, you can infect them with your enthusiasm and demonstrate how easy and fun these workshops really are.

Team

You'll need a team of instructors that can present the different workshops. Contact your local (Java) User Group, organize a preparation meeting, get your partner involved, and invite your friends and family. Ask your son or daughter to invite friends from school and talk to their parents. Devoxx is a community conference, so reach out and get everybody involved.

Registration

The D4K events are organized with a nonprofit mentality. Thus, the first D4K event in Belgium was free. However, we soon realized that on sunny weekends, 30% would not show up, because families prefer to go to the beach instead (and rightly so). But from an organization point of view, this doesn't really help. Asking a small fee, like $10, resulted in a 95% attendance rate. We use EventBrite (*http://www.eventbrite.com*), which can easily be configured, and after their commission fee, you still have enough to provide each child with a nice D4K T-shirt and serve some drinks and fruit during the breaks.

Bring Your Own

Children should bring their own lunch, which makes it easy for everyone. But as an organization, do provide enough drinks, fruit, and cookies so these hungry minds have enough energy to digest the information.

Parents Track

Arun Gupta holds a parallel parent track in San Francisco where he debriefs the parents on what the children will see during the day. This is a great way to teach all parties involved, and often results in a parent champion, who can answer their children's follow-up questions once they are back home. You will be the star of the week if you can help your teenage child!

Some countries also demand that a parent is present during a child-driven workshop, so the approach with the partners track solves both requirements.

Parent Waiver

Make sure you write down the mobile number of the parent(s), especially if they don't stay. In addition, require parents to sign a parental waiver that allows you to take pictures or even make an atmosphere video of the event. Again, some countries demand this; check locally if this is required.

Promo Video

Make sure to create your own promo/atmosphere video. Invite a local media company or students—they will love to help and can turn it into a special project.

In Belgium, I invited Roy van Rijn, who's a real magician when it comes to capturing the moment, and his video (*https://vimeo.com/51393678*) was clearly a big help to spread the word and enthusiasm of the very first D4K event.

We even received a very nice animated intro video from Devoxx4Kids Nantes, which we now use as our default intro video.

Press

A quote I picked up during Devoxx France at the annual JUG BOF: "I've been organizing a Java User Group for the last 10 years and never saw a journalist. Last month we did a D4K event for 50 children and we were on national television!"

It shows that this is a hot topic that is receiving lots of attention from the press. There is this problem and we're offering a (small) solution. Reach out and be astonished!

For more information, see the press page (*http://www.devoxx4kids.org/press-media/*).

Sponsors

More and more companies are excited to sponsor this initiative. Some will offer their offices, like universities and schools; others offer merchandising assistance; and some even provide a financial donation. For example, Oracle Academy and Red Hat have been huge supporters of D4K and have financially supported this initiative, allowing us to purchase our own Lego Mindstorms and even T-shirts for the instructors and children. Thank you!

Create a win-win situation for all parties involved and you'll see the sky is the limit. Explore and be amazed.

Agile Teams

Have the children work in pairs and have them switch between workshops. This is a great way to improve their social skills, but also get them introduced to pair development, which is of course encouraged when doing agile development.

And last but not least: have fun!

It should be a fun day for the children, but also for you and other parents. Try to move around and even try to follow some workshops—you'll be amazed how smart and fast these kids are.

Make sure you get a good night's rest the day before: you'll be exhausted after the workshop, but will have a big smile on your face because these events are both emotionally and intellectually very rewarding!

The Future of Devoxx4Kids?

D4K has only started scratching the surface of how technology needs to be enabled for kids around the world. Where do we go from here?

Workshop Translations

Our workshops (freely available on GitHub) are already translated from English to French, Dutch, Italian, and German. In the near future, more workshops and even more translations are expected as new D4K chapters are started around the world.

If we can complement the workshops with more in-depth online courses, we can deliver a powerful learning path for the knowledge-hungry, enthusiastic children!

More and Bigger

For the D4K chapters that have already organized one or two events, we're seeing a clear trend that they're starting to raise the bar by organizing more frequent and bigger events. For example, D4K San Francisco organizes events on a biweekly basis. Some are taking it to the next level with sponsors, and holding workshops for hundreds of children. We can only encourage this—if the system is broken, then let's lead by example.

Online Courses

An amazing opportunity in the D4K evolution will be to leverage the Parleys.com platform (which is used by Devoxx to publish the rich media presentations). I'd love to introduce online courses on this platform in different languages so that children can continue their D4K enthusiasm and learn more about a certain topic at their own pace, wherever, whenever.

It's very obvious that more and more people will receive an online certificate/diploma without ever physically entering the school premises. We can live wherever on this planet and get an online education, but the challenge will be to balance our needed social contacts, making real friends, and looking beyond the screen—not easy.

Index

Thaumcraft mod, 128
The End dimension, 132
ticks
    about, 40
    setting item lifespan in, 42
TNT explosions
    bigger, 38-43
    primed TNT and, 39
    TNT bombs, 37, 82
    with fuses, 40-43
    without fuses, 38-39
tools
    about, 1, 146
    downloading and installing, 2-9
    location of, 147
    for making textures, 116
    types of, 146
transforming blocks and items
    about, 141
    brewing, 144
    crafting, 141-142
    smelting, 143
transparencies, 117
trapdoors, 140
try-catch statement, 72, 80

U

unlocalized names, 86

V

variables
    about, 11
    adding to main file, 19
    storing decimals, 38
verifying mods, 13-14, 25, 89
verifying textures, 122

W

Weakness potion, 145
wheat, 141
wood (tool material), 146
wood logs, 141
wooden planks, 141, 144
workshops (Deevoxx4Kids), 156-162
workspaces, 7
worlds
    changing names of, 138
    creating new, 137, 147
    testing mods in, 25

Z

ZIP files, 5
zombies
    about, 49, 145
    spawning with armor, 30, 49-51
    zombie knights, 49-51
Zoom tool, 116

About the Authors

Arun Gupta is a founding member of Devoxx4Kids USA. As a chair of the board, he oversees the operation of this nonprofit organization and ensures it stays true to its mission of promoting technology education among kids. After completing a master's in computer science, he moved to the United States many years ago and enjoys the beautiful California weather with his lovely wife and two boys. During the day, he works as director of developer advocacy at Red Hat and focuses on JBoss Middleware. He has spent several years building and coaching middleware applications at Sun Microsystems and Oracle. Arun has extensive speaking experience in about 40 countries on myriad topics and is a JavaOne Rock Star. An author of a best-selling book, an avid runner, a globe-trotter, a Java champion, and a Silicon Valley JUG leader, he is easily accessible on Twitter (*@arungupta*).

Aditya Gupta is a 12-year-old middle schooler at Moreland Middle School, San Jose, California. He loves to play and modify Minecraft. He also has experience in many other types of programming, including Scratch, Java, Python, Greenfoot, and iOS. At age 11, he was one of the youngest speakers ever at the Community Keynote of JavaOne 2013, showing how pigs fly using Eclipse in front of 1,500+ Java developers. He builds and delivers workshops for Devoxx4Kids, and is excited to teach programming skills to young kids like himself. He is also a Boy Scout and enjoys tinkering with Legos.

Colophon

The animal on the cover of *Minecraft Modding with Forge* is a Texas horned lizard (*Phrynosoma cornutum*), known colloquially as a "horny toad." Though it has a short snout and flattened body that looks similar to a frog or toad, it is in fact a reptile. This is one of 14 horned lizard species, and is the most widespread with a range throughout the southwestern United States and northern Mexico (particularly in the Sonoran desert). It is the state reptile of Texas.

The Texas horned lizard has a distinctive "crown" of horns on its head, the number and pattern of which varies between species. These horns are extensions of the animal's skull, and are made of true bone. The average length of these lizards is 2.7 inches, though females tend to be larger than males. Their scales are tan with dark splotches (which serve as camouflage), and there are rows of small spikes on their back and sides.

While the horned lizard eats various insects, red harvester ants make up nearly 70% of its diet. Both the ant and the lizard prefer warmer temperatures, so are often active at the same time of day. However, the horned lizard population has recently declined, perhaps because their primary food source has become harder to find: the increased use of pesticides and spread of the aggressive fire ant species have wiped out many harvester ant colonies.

While the Texas horned lizard does not have many natural predators, it has several defensive tactics. When threatened, it will puff its body up, making its scales protrude and becoming harder to swallow. It is a capable digger, and can quickly burrow underground to escape threats. It is also able to squirt a stream of blood from its eyes, up to 5 feet away. Not only does this confuse predators, but the blood contains a chemical that tastes particularly bad to canines (like wolves, coyotes, and domestic dogs).

Many of the animals on O'Reilly covers are endangered; all of them are important to the world. To learn more about how you can help, go to *animals.oreilly.com*.

The cover image is from *Meyers Kleines Lexicon*. The cover fonts are URW Typewriter and Guardian Sans. The text font is Adobe Minion Pro; the heading font is Adobe Myriad Condensed; and the code font is Dalton Maag's Ubuntu Mono.

Get even more for your money.

Join the O'Reilly Community, and register the O'Reilly books you own. It's free, and you'll get:

- $4.99 ebook upgrade offer
- 40% upgrade offer on O'Reilly print books
- Membership discounts on books and events
- Free lifetime updates to ebooks and videos
- Multiple ebook formats, DRM FREE
- Participation in the O'Reilly community
- Newsletters
- Account management
- 100% Satisfaction Guarantee

Signing up is easy:

1. Go to: oreilly.com/go/register
2. Create an O'Reilly login.
3. Provide your address.
4. Register your books.

Note: English-language books only

To order books online:
oreilly.com/store

For questions about products or an order:
orders@oreilly.com

To sign up to get topic-specific email announcements and/or news about upcoming books, conferences, special offers, and new technologies:
elists@oreilly.com

For technical questions about book content:
booktech@oreilly.com

To submit new book proposals to our editors:
proposals@oreilly.com

O'Reilly books are available in multiple DRM-free ebook formats. For more information:
oreilly.com/ebooks

CPSIA information can be obtained at www.ICGtesting.com
Printed in the USA
BVOW09s1622020415

394500BV00002B/3/P